Neighbors and
Ne'er-Do-Wells

Neighbors and Ne'er-Do-Wells

Two Parables of Amazing Love as Told by Jesus

To my friend Carlo—
May this prove to be a blessing
to you and those around you.

D. H. Shearer

WestBow
PRESS
A DIVISION OF THOMAS NELSON

Copyright © 2013 D. H. Shearer.

All rights reserved. No part of this book may be used or reproduced by any means, graphic, electronic, or mechanical, including photocopying, recording, taping or by any information storage retrieval system without the written permission of the publisher except in the case of brief quotations embodied in critical articles and reviews.

WestBow Press books may be ordered through booksellers or by contacting:

WestBow Press
A Division of Thomas Nelson
1663 Liberty Drive
Bloomington, IN 47403
www.westbowpress.com
1-(866) 928-1240

Because of the dynamic nature of the Internet, any web addresses or links contained in this book may have changed since publication and may no longer be valid. The views expressed in this work are solely those of the author and do not necessarily reflect the views of the publisher, and the publisher hereby disclaims any responsibility for them.

Any people depicted in stock imagery provided by Thinkstock are models, and such images are being used for illustrative purposes only.

Certain stock imagery © Thinkstock.

ISBN: 978-1-4497-8843-8 (sc)
ISBN: 978-1-4497-8842-1 (e)

Library of Congress Control Number: 2013904558

Printed in the United States of America

WestBow Press rev. date: 03/21/2013

Table of Contents

Preface: An Invitation to *Neighbors and Ne'er-Do-Wells* vii

Introduction
    Chapter 1:   The Power of Parables 1

Part 1: The Parable of the Good Samaritan
    Chapter 2:   Approaching the Parable of the
                    Good Samaritan 12
    Chapter 3:   The Attorney and His Agenda 25
    Chapter 4:   Crime and Compassion 42
    Chapter 5:   The Answer and Some Applications 59

Part 2: The Parable of the Prodigal Son
    Chapter 6:   Approaching the Parable of the
                    Prodigal Son 76
    Chapter 7:   The Seduction of Sin 86
    Chapter 8:   The Role of Repentance 102
    Chapter 9:   In the Grip of Grace 113
    Chapter 10: Grumbling About Grace 127
    Chapter 11: The Result of Reconciliation 142

Epilogue
    Chapter 12: Morals to the Stories 155

An Invitation to
Neighbors and Ne'er-Do-Wells

Everybody loves a good story. Whether we're talking about something that we did with our friends last week or something that happened unexpectedly during a church service, people are social creatures. We love to tell stories about things that happened, or even things that didn't happen. In America, more books about fiction are published each year than any other genre.

While not a novelist, Jesus was nevertheless a master story teller! In fact, at one point Jesus taught exclusively by means of parables. (Matthew 13:34) But Jesus didn't tell stories simply to entertain those who were listening. He understood that a good story is like a window that lets light in. A good story illuminates and helps us to understand truth more clearly.

As a preaching pastor, I realize that it's the stories that people remember the most in my sermons. In fact, people often remember stories long after they have forgotten a catchy title or outline. Stories have "staying power." A good story isn't easily forgotten. That's because they have a tendency to draw us into them, causing us to reflect on where we find ourselves within their scope. A good story isn't just something that we hear. It's something that we experience.

This book is primarily about two stories that Jesus told—stories that have incredible staying power. The Parables of the Good Samaritan and the Prodigal Son are about "amazing love." They both speak volumes about our interpersonal relationships in our families, our churches, and even among nations. The main text may be read by itself. Those wishing to dig a bit deeper will find sources and issues of a more academic nature addressed in the endnotes at the end of the book. Discussion questions are also provided at the close of each chapter to spur additional thinking for individuals and groups.

Neighbors and Ne'er-Do-Wells is based on a series of lectures I presented under the auspices of South Seas Christian Ministries to future church leaders and pastors at Malua Theological College in Western Samoa. They've also been kindly received by Turner Christian Church in Turner, Oregon, where I'm privileged to serve as their pastor. My thanks and appreciation is extended to my friends on both sides of the Pacific Ocean.

May God add his blessing as we enter into these two great stories and allow His Spirit to challenge us.

D. H. Shearer
Turner, Oregon
February, 2013

Chapter 1
The Power of Parables

Jesus was an incredible story teller! He knew how a good story not only creates interest, but can be instructive as well. Jesus also knew how to masterfully craft a story by taking into consideration his faith, culture, environment, and social mores. The result is that some of the most powerful and memorable teachings we have from Jesus have been passed down to us in story form.

Still, when Jesus told stories he was not inventing a new genre or method of teaching. The parable was already widely known and popular before Jesus was born. In ancient Greece and Rome parables were routinely used by politicians, philosophers, religious teachers and even lawyers. In fact, the Greek word rendered in many newer translations as "lawyer" in Acts 24:1 (*rhētōr*) is the root of the word rhetoric. (Acts 24:1) These professionals, trained in the art of effective oratory, argued cases in court using all their powers of persuasion. The power of a good illustrative story no doubt won many cases.

Both Socrates and Aristotle utilized parables as teaching tools. In his book *The Art of Rhetoric,* Aristotle devoted an entire section to how parables can be used in persuasive speech.[1] Interestingly, while Aristotle wrote about the effective use of parables, he also believed that such "verbal beauty" was an inborn talent and a skill that could never be fully taught.

As Aristotle's influence spread throughout the known world, so did his teaching on rhetoric. Using parables as a means of teaching and persuasion was well established by the time of Jesus.

Here's just one example of how powerfully a well-crafted story is used in the Old Testament. In 2 Samuel 2:1-7 Nathan speaks to King David about his sin with Bathsheba. Rather than confronting him directly, Nathan instead tells a story about a rich man who steals a poor man's beloved lamb. The lamb is just about the only thing of value that the poor man owns. In addition, it is more than merely a family pet. It is like a member of his family. At any rate, the rich man steals it, butchers it, and serves it to his guests for dinner.

When David hears the story, he is outraged. His sense of justice is violated. How dare that rich man steal the poor man's beloved lamb, especially when he has so many other lambs in his own flocks from which to choose! "The man who did this must die!" David cries, "He must pay for that lamb four times over, because he did such a thing and had no pity." Nathan answers, "You are the man." (2 Samuel 12:5-7) Nathan goes on to explain David's abuse of power when he stole Bathsheba, the wife of Uriah. By confronting David by means of a parable, Nathan drew him into the story in such a way that David ended up condemning himself for his own behavior.[2]

What is a Parable?

The word "parable" is a compound word. Literally, *parabolē* means "that which is thrown beside" (*para*= "alongside"; *ballō*= "to throw"). A parable is illustrative material that is added to strengthen the force of what's being said.

Broadly speaking, a parable is any "dark saying." It's not dark in the sense of being sinister, but rather it's something that's not intended to be taken at face value. The truth lies *beyond* the parable. The story itself is a work of fiction. So, for example, in the Parable of the Sower when Jesus says, "A farmer went out to sow his seed," (Matthew 13:3) the farmer is not a person who actually lived. The truth of the story in lies in its meaning, not in its historicity.

Types of Parables

For the sake of clarity, we observe that there are four different types of parables in the New Testament.[3] First, a parable might be simply a proverb or wise saying. At one point Jesus says, "Surely you will quote this proverb to me: 'Physician, heal yourself!'" (Luke 4:23) In the original Greek text, however, the word for proverb is *parabolē*. While we might not think of proverbs and parables as being synonymous, in this case they are.

On other occasions a parable might be nothing more than a thought provoking question. When Jesus is accused of being possessed by Beelzebub he responds by asking a question, which the Gospel of Mark calls a parable. We read, "So Jesus called them over to him and began to speak to them in parables: 'How can Satan drive out Satan? If a kingdom is divided against itself, that kingdom cannot stand.'" (Mark 3:23-24) Another example takes place during the Sermon on the Plain, where the Gospel of Luke records, "He also told them this parable: 'Can the blind lead the blind? Will they not both fall into a pit?'" (Luke 6:39)[4]

Sometimes an illustration of something is called a parable. In Hebrews 9 the writer explains that the high priest entered into the

Holy Place once a year, offering a sacrifice for both his sins and for the sins of the people. The writer concludes that such a sacrifice was necessary because a permanent solution for sin had not yet come. Then he says, "This is an illustration (*parabolē*) for the present time." (Hebrews 9:9) Later in Hebrews, the writer speaks of Abraham's sacrifice of Isaac, the "child of promise." "Abraham reasoned that God could even raise the dead, and so in a manner of speaking he did receive Isaac back from death." (Hebrews 11:19) Literally it says that Abraham received Isaac "in parable."[5] In other words, there's a message here that reaches beyond the story of Abraham and Isaac. Abraham's sacrifice of Isaac foreshadowed the time when God would offer up his Son, Jesus, on a cross and receive him back from the dead.

But by far the most common way in which parables are employed is found in the synoptic gospels. They are short, fictional stories designed to convey truths beyond the stories themselves, which is what most of us think of when we think of parables. Roughly a third of Jesus' recorded total teaching was done through parables. Of the 50 times where the word "parable" appears in the New Testament, 48 of them are in the synoptic gospels of Matthew, Mark, and Luke.

It's hard to determine exactly how many parables Jesus told. The four gospels simply do not give us a complete record of everything that Jesus said and did. Indeed, the Apostle John surmises that if everything that Jesus ever said and did were written down, the whole world could not contain all of the books that would have to be written. (John 20:25)

Another factor making it difficult to determine how many parables Jesus told is that scholars don't agree as to what precisely constitutes a parable. There are 30 places where Jesus' words are specifically called parables. Beyond that, however, there are another

10 teachings of Jesus that could be considered parables, depending upon your definition and criteria. Plus, we could add another 25 if we included such broad sayings as "Do not throw your pearls to pigs." (Matthew 7:6) In short, depending upon how they are counted, the gospels record as many as 65 different parables taught by Jesus.

The Purpose of Parables

Why did Jesus tell stories so often? As the Apostle Matthew reflected on the life of Jesus, he saw the fulfillment of Old Testament prophecy in many instances. The Psalmist wrote, "I will open my mouth with a parable; I will utter hidden things, things from of old." (Psalm 78:2) Remembering this verse, Matthew wrote, "Jesus spoke all these things to the crowd in parables; he did not say anything to them without using a parable. So was fulfilled what was spoken through the prophet: 'I will open my mouth in parables, I will utter things hidden since the creation of the world.'" (Matthew 13:34-36)

But to say that Jesus told parables in order to fulfill prophecy puts the proverbial "cart before the horse." A better understanding is that Jesus told parables and Matthew saw in Jesus what the psalmist had written. In other words, Jesus didn't tell parables in order to fulfill prophecy. Rather, the prophecy was given because Jesus would tell parables. The prophecies were "fulfilled" in Jesus.[6] That is, the prophetic words found their fullness (i.e. they were "filled full" of meaning) in Jesus. To be sure, they had meaning before Jesus came, but their *full* meaning can only be understood in the light of Christ. In short, Jesus is the key to

> Jesus didn't tell parables in order to fulfill prophecy. Rather, the prophecy was given because Jesus would tell parables.

understanding Old Testament prophecy. He is the starting point. Only when our eyes are fixed firmly on Jesus are we able to understand the Old Testament in all of its rich fullness.

Of course, a primary reason that Jesus told parables was to explain truth in a concrete way. It's often been said that a parable is "an earthly story with a heavenly meaning." While there's certainly some truth in that old saying, it doesn't go nearly far enough. While some of the stories that Jesus told did focus on heaven, the majority of them were about how we live our lives here and now.

In short, while it might be difficult to grasp abstract concepts, parables are drawn from everyday life experiences.[7] Whether it's a sower who goes forth to sow his seed, a woman who kneads her dough while making bread, or a fisherman lowering his dragnet, these stories are derived from situations that most hearers can readily understand, thus starting us all on common ground. And because we all begin at a common level of understanding, there's always a sense of "What does this parable say to you?" As Richard Jensen observes, "The listener is grasped by the reality of the story through the story itself."[8]

There is a danger, however. Whenever parables are retold to people who live in different cultural contexts, much of the impact of "common ground" can be lost. While the initial hearers of Jesus' parables were well versed in their culture, most western Christians are not. When modern, urban American hears Jesus' story about a shepherd leaving 99 sheep in the dangerous open country to go in search of the one sheep who was lost (Luke 15:3-7), they might require the dynamics of the situation to be explained to them. Or when a modern housewife hears of a woman who owns ten silver coins and loses one (Luke 15:8-10), she might not understand the special value such a coin might have.

It's often been observed that a parable is like a joke: either you get it or you don't. If you don't get it, someone can still explain it to you, but it will never have the same impact it would have had had you understood it in the first place. Still, these stories imprint an important image in our mind's eye, helping us to see abstract truth more concretely.

An advantage in using parables as a teaching technique is that they allow students to discover truth for themselves. The power of self-discovery is undeniable. When the listener can put "two and two" together and come up with a proper response, the impact is much greater and more memorable than if a teacher had merely given the answer.

Of course, it is possible that the listener will draw wrong conclusions based on the parable. So the great strength of parables is also their weakness. Great discernment is required. It is very easy for an interpreter to impose his or her own bias and agenda upon the text.

Parables are also a great teaching tool because they hold our interest. They are not long, drawn out lectures that could easily become dry and boring. Instead, they almost have a life of their own as they draw us into them. It's hard to daydream when you're engulfed in a story, wondering how it all might end.

This is especially true with the parables of Jesus. Jesus' stories often have a surprise within them, a twist in the story or something shocking that you weren't expecting. In the Parable of the Prodigal Son, it's shocking that a younger son would be so insolent as to demand his share of the inheritance even before his father had died, or that his father would welcome him home so freely. (Luke 15:11-32) In the Parable of the Sower, it's shocking that the seed would be cast out so indiscriminately. (Matthew 13:3-8) Imagine the snub when invited guests to a wedding banquet refuse to come, or the rude way in which those who finally attend are dressed. (Matthew 22:1-14) Or how about the way in which a crooked money manager who had recently been fired shrewdly used his employer's wealth to gain his own future financial security? (Luke 16:1-9)

Sometimes Jesus surprised his listeners by using hyperbole, exaggerating in order to make a point. In the Parable of the Unmerciful Servant, the first servant owed his master 10,000 talents, the amount of money that a laborer could expect to earn in 150,000 years. No one could possibly pay off such a debt. In contrast, the second servant only owed 100 denarii, or about three months' worth of labor. (Matthew 18:21-35)

On other occasions the shock comes through a reversal of sympathies. A Pharisee and a hated tax collector go up to the temple to pray, but it is the tax collector who is justified in the end. (Luke 18:9-14) Or consider who the hero turns out to be in the Parable of the Good Samaritan. (Luke 10:25-37)

And finally, we must remember that all of the parables Jesus told were originally given in verbal form. It wasn't until many years later that they were written down. Because parables were originally given orally, they could be employed in virtually any setting—in church, at the dinner table, or even at the beach. Furthermore, while things in print are often dissected word for word and point by point, oral stories are rarely received that way. They tend to be heard more as a whole. As a consequence, parables generally have only a very limited number of applications that are in keeping with the speaker's original purpose.

Revealing, Yet Concealing

Still, not every parable was designed to reveal God's truth to everyone. Jesus himself acknowledged that the very vehicle used to convey truth can also obscure it. When his disciples asked Jesus why he spoke to the people in parables, he replied it was "because the knowledge of the secrets of the kingdom of heaven has been given to you, but not to them . . . This is why I speak to them in parables: 'Though seeing, they do not see; though hearing, they do not hear or understand.'" (Matthew 13:11, 13) Jesus' words are even stronger in Mark 4:12 and Luke 8:10, where he said he spoke in parables so that "they may be ever seeing but never perceiving, and ever hearing but never understanding."

Some of parables, while offered publicly, were like a confidential conversation. What was said was not necessarily intended for everyone to hear or understand. Whether a particular parable Jesus told was intended to be understood by everyone— whether it would reveal or conceal the message—depended upon the audience. For example, when Jesus spoke about the kingdom of God, he realized that the Romans who occupied Israel might consider his teaching a threat to their empire. So Jesus spoke about the smallest of all the seeds, a mustard seed.[9] Despite its small size it grows to become the largest of garden plants.[10] Those with spiritual discernment would understand that while the kingdom would start small, it would eventually grow to an immense and nurturing size. To those without such discernment, the story was nothing but a brief lesson on agriculture.

Still, Jesus obviously intended his parables to be understood or why else would he say, "Whoever has ears, let them hear?" (Matthew 13:9) And why would he later feel the need to explain some of his parables to his disciples?

The ultimate responsibility for understanding parables, then, rests with the hearer, rather than with the story teller. Twenty-two of Jesus' parables begin with the words "Who among you . . . ?" or "What do you think . . . ?" The listener is put on notice from the very beginning that he needs to draw a conclusion when the story is over. Therefore, parables are not just about what Jesus thinks. They are also about how his thinking affects our thinking when we properly apply them.

Jesus says, "In them [those who fail to understand the message] is fulfilled the prophecy of Isaiah:[11]

> 'You will be ever hearing but never understanding;
> you will be ever seeing but never perceiving.
> For this people's heart has become calloused;
> they hardly hear with their ears,
> and they have closed their eyes.
> Otherwise they might see with their eyes,
> hear with their ears,
> understand with their hearts
> and turn, and I would heal them.'" (Matthew 13:14-15)

Why do some people continue to reject the truth, even after numerous opportunities to hear the good news? Ultimately it is a heart problem, causing them to hardly hear any more, or to see with clarity. As a result, there is no understanding.

Jesus concludes, "But blessed are your eyes because they see, and your ears because they hear. For truly I tell you, many prophets and righteous people longed to see what you see but did not see it, and to hear what you hear but did not hear it." (Matthew 13:16-17) Those who understand these parables are blessed indeed. For even the most righteous of Old Testament heroes did not have the access to these great teachings of Jesus that we enjoy.

Our Focus

Together we will explore two of Jesus' most famous parables. The Parable of the Good Samaritan (Luke 10:25-37) speaks of the Christian's obligation to be a neighbor to all people. It is chosen because of the far-reaching implications it has in our dealings, not just with those who live near to us, but in faraway cultures as well. As America becomes more ethnically diverse, the relevance of this parable for Christians becomes all the more pertinent.

The second parable is the story of the Prodigal Son. (Luke 15:11-32) This parable is selected because of its pointed emphasis on interpersonal relationships within our human families and within God's family, the church. To live in harmony with God demands that we live in harmony with one another.

Discussion

1. What stories or experiences from your childhood, parents, or ancestors have influenced how you see yourself today?
2. The author writes, "The truth of the story lies in its meaning, not in its historicity." Do you think this always the case? Why or why not?
3. Why do you think the Gospel of John is so silent when it comes to recording Jesus' parables?
4. How did Jesus' parables fulfill prophecy? (Matthew 13:34-36) Can you identify any other prophecies about Jesus that were fulfilled in the same general way?
5. Given the fact that a parable can be understood in so many different ways, why do you think Jesus would be willing to run the risk of misinterpretation?

Chapter 2

Approaching the Parable of the Good Samaritan

The Parable of the Good Samaritan is one of the best known and most loved stories that Jesus told. This chapter addresses some introductory issues about the parable. First we'll examine the generally positive way in which Samaritans are perceived today, in contrast to how they were viewed in the days of Jesus. We'll note three different ways (or levels) in which passages like this one have historically been understood. And finally, we'll see how the interpreter's life experience, values, and social context can influence the way in which this parable, or any passage of Scripture, is understood.

Because the Parable of the Good Samaritan is so well known, our familiarity with it presents some unique challenges. For instance, we might stop listening whenever the story is read, thinking that we already know how the story goes. Or perhaps we've heard the story so many times that its impact is all but lost. We've become so familiar with the plot and the characters that we've almost domesticated them.

Present Perceptions

Take the term "Samaritan" for instance. In American society a Good Samaritan is generally thought of as someone who helps someone else in a time of need—someone who demonstrates mercy and compassion—perhaps even at a substantial risk or cost to himself. So when we think of a Samaritan, we generally think of it in decidedly positive terms. In fact, we even admire such people for their unselfish generosity.

It's therefore not unusual to find the name "Good Samaritan" linked to all sorts of things. Numerous hospitals and churches carry the name. There's a Roman Catholic order of nuns called "The Sisters of the Good Samaritan." Franklin Graham heads an international ministry called "Samaritan's Purse." Perhaps there's a "Good Samaritan School" not far from where you live. Presumably it's a place where among other things children learn to be kind, to share and to get along with others. There's even a Good Samaritan ointment on the market for "cuts, scrapes, burns, dry cracked skin and skin irritations." But no matter how the term "Samaritan" or "Good Samaritan" is used, it is certainly viewed in a positive light today.

In addition, there are so-called "Good Samaritan Laws." Let's suppose that you're out taking a walk one day and you come across someone who's been in a terrible automobile accident. The driver of the car is unconscious and bleeding badly. Now, you're not a physician or an Emergency Medical Technician. You have no formal training. But you have to do something or else the person will bleed to death.

But wait! What if you unintentionally do something to this victim that actually makes his situation worse? Remember, you have no formal medical training. As terrible as it sounds, some people might rather have the person bleed to death than to run the risk of being taken to court for making his condition worse. The

Good Samaritan Law simply says that if you're doing your best to help someone in an emergency situation like this, then you can't be prosecuted. You're protected, so you are free to render whatever aid you might be able to provide.

But again, the term "Samaritan" or "Good Samaritan" is generally seen in a positive light. So when we read the story of the Good Samaritan in the Bible, we might jump to the natural conclusion that the Samaritan must be the hero.

Past Perceptions

But is that how those who first heard Jesus tell this story understood it? By no means! To them, a Samaritan was someone who had a racially and religiously mixed ancestry. When the Northern Kingdom of Israel was overrun by the Assyrians in 722 B.C., a relatively small number of Jews were left behind and not taken off into captivity. As a result, they intermarried with the existing pagan population and with Assyrian settlers sent to colonize the area. They generally lived in the region of Samaria. (2 Kings 17:24-41)

When the full-blooded Jews returned to Israel, these Samaritans were not allowed to help in the rebuilding the Temple in Jerusalem. In response, they solidified their own commitment to Mount Gerizim by building their own Temple there. In the mind of most Jews, the Samaritans were unclean, socially outcaste, and religiously heretical. They were hated by the full-blooded Jews in the days of Jesus.[1]

The Fourth Gospel tells the story of Jesus meeting with a woman of Samaria at Jacob's well. As John tells the story, Jesus asks the woman for a drink, which catches her by surprise. John then feels the need to explain that "Jews do not associate with Samaritans." (John 4:9)

In fact, calling someone a "Samaritan" was a bit of an epithet—even a curse word. A Samaritan was someone who wasn't orthodox. It is significant that at one point Jesus himself was called both a Samaritan and demon possessed. (John 8:48)

To call someone a "Good Samaritan," therefore, was a contradiction. As far as the Jews were concerned, you could be *good,* or you could be a *Samaritan,* but you couldn't possibly be both. There were no "Good Samaritans!"

The Parable of the Good Samaritan must have been truly offensive to the lawyer who prompted it. Given his cultural background, he would have certainly expected the Samaritan to be the villain in this story and would have anticipated the heroes to be the priest and the Levite. Instead, Jesus turns everything upside down. In fact, at the end of this parable the lawyer won't even be willing to utter the word "Samaritan" when Jesus asks him which one proved to be a neighbor. (Luke 10:37)

> Calling someone a "Samaritan" was a bit of an epithet—even a curse word.

Interpreting Parables

Before we look closely at the Parable of the Good Samaritan itself, it will be helpful to examine the various ways in which parables (and this parable in particular) have historically been interpreted.

Origen was a student of Clement, who is sometimes called "the first full-time Christian scholar." Origen lived about 150 years after Jesus and was at the forefront of the Alexandrian school of interpretation. He argued that there are really three different levels at which you can interpret any passage of scripture.[2]

The first is the *physical* (or literal) level. In the case of the Parable of the Good Samaritan, the physical level would take this story literally, on face value. That is, a lawyer asks Jesus what he has to do in order to inherit eternal life. When his exchange with Jesus proves unsatisfactory, he asks "Who is my neighbor?" Jesus answers by telling a story, illustrating that a neighbor is anyone who demonstrates mercy. In other words, the *physical* level concerns itself with such issues as who the Samaritans were, the role of priests and Levites, the dangerous route the man who fell among robbers was traveling, the medicinal nature of oil and wine, and so forth.

The second level probes a bit deeper into the story. Origen called this the *psychic* level. The psychic level focuses on the moral lessons that can be drawn from the text. As Craig Blomberg analyzes the Parable of the Good Samaritan, he draws several moral conclusions that illustrate this *psychic* approach.[3] According to Blomberg, the primary lesson is that Christians are called to show compassion to anyone who's in need. Obviously that's the case, because when confronted with the mercy demonstrated by the Samaritan, the lawyer is told to "Go and do likewise." (Luke 10:37) And clearly we're supposed to emulate the Samaritan's example every bit as much as the lawyer was supposed to.

But go and do *what* likewise? Answering that question is what the *psychic* level of interpretation is all about. Does this teaching only apply to you when coming across someone who has been stripped, beaten, robbed, and left for dead? That's what a strict, *physical* (or literal) interpretation would require. If you should ever come across someone who's in such a dire position you should immediately go a search for a donkey, buy some oil and wine, and take him to a motel, and expect to pay the bill with only two silver coins. But such a narrow application is rather ridiculous, isn't it?

The *psychic* level asks the question, "How can I apply this teaching to my situation?" Maybe the person in need hasn't been beaten and robbed. Maybe instead he's too sick to work and his family is hungry. Maybe he's been laid off from a job he's held for 20 years and his house is now in foreclosure. Maybe he's a college student who can't afford a textbook, the one in the library is checked out, and he'd like to borrow your copy. Does it matter if you know the person in need or not? What if he's close to you? Does that raise the level of your responsibility?

Maybe you're not independently wealthy and could never afford to help someone financially, but you *do* have the ability to help him pack in the event of an eviction. This is the *psychic* level of interpretation. It asks the question, "How does this passage of scripture apply to my specific situation?"

But there are other moral questions we can ask. Since the hero in the story is a hated Samaritan, does that mean that even my enemies should be treated as neighbors?" Is there a hierarchy in terms of my responsibility to help others? Perhaps family and close friends come first, then people in my church, then those in my community, then strangers, then last of all, my enemies. Is that how benevolence is supposed to work in the kingdom?

And finally, Origen said there's a third, even deeper level of interpretation, which is the *mystical* (or allegorical) level. An allegory is a literary device where literal meanings are dismissed and the characters in a story represent something entirely different. Each character or item in the parable stands for something else. But we must be very careful here.

Jesus told some parables that are clearly allegorical in nature. For example, in the Parable of Sower a farmer goes forth to sow his seed. (Matthew 13:3-9) The seed flies in every direction. It falls on the path, on rocky places, among thorns, and on good soil. Starting in Matthew 13:18, Jesus interprets this parable, using allegory. The story is not about antiquated farming methods. Rather, it is about how people respond to the gospel.

The path represents those who don't understand the message, so it never takes root. The rocky places stands for those who receive the word, but because of persecution will later reject it. The thorns are those who receive the word, but when the troubles of life take over, with the deceitfulness of wealth, the seed is rendered unfruitful. But the good soil stands for those who hear, understand, obey, and reproduce. Each aspect of the parable represents something beyond itself.

An allegorical approach works well in the Parable of the Sower, especially since Jesus himself interpreted it in such a way. There are also other examples of allegorical parables, such as the Parable of the Weeds in the Field (Matthew 13:24-30) and the Parable of the Wicked Tenants (Matthew 21:33-44).

But what about the Parable of the Good Samaritan? Here's how Augustine of Hippo (354-430 A.D.) interpreted the parable, using the *mystical* (or allegorical) method. To Augustine, the story is emblematic of the story of redemption. The man who falls among robbers is Adam, who represents the entire human race. Having been expelled from the Heavenly Jerusalem, he now travels downhill to Jericho, which is emblematic of his own mortality. The robbers are the Devil and his angels. The priest and the Levite represent the ministry under the Old Covenant, which was powerless to save. The Samaritan stands for Jesus Christ, who binds up the man's wounds (that is, his sinful estate) with oil and wine, which is hope and encouragement. He places him on his own animal, which is belief in the incarnation. He takes him to the inn, which is the church. On the next day (the time after the resurrection), he takes out two coins, emblematic of love and the promise of everlasting life, and pays the debt that's owed—the atonement. And the innkeeper is none other than the Apostle Paul, a faithful servant of the church, who is charged with the ongoing care of the man.[4]

John Newton, who wrote the popular hymn *Amazing Grace,* also interpreted the Parable of the Good Samaritan allegorically. He summarized the parable in poetic form, putting himself in the place of the man who fell among the thieves:

> How kind the Good Samaritan
> To him who fell among the thieves!
> Thus Jesus pities fallen man,
> And heals the wounds the soul receives.
>
> O! I remember well the day,
> When sorely wounded, nearly slain;
> Like that poor man I bleeding lay,
> And groaned for help, but groaned in vain.
>
> Men saw me in this helpless case,
> And passed without compassion by;
> Each neighbor turned away his face,
> Unmoved by my mournful cry.
>
> But he whose name had been my scorn,
> As Jews Samaritans despise
> Came, when he saw me thus forlorn,
> With love and pity in his eyes.
>
> Gently he raised me from the ground,
> Pressed me to lean upon his arm;
> And into every gaping wound
> He poured his own all-healing balm.

> Unto his church my steps he led,
> The house prepared for sinners lost;
> Gave charge I should be clothed and fed;
> And took upon him all the cost.
>
> Thus saved from death, from want secured,
> I wait till he again shall come,
> When I shall be completely cured
> And take me to his heav'nly home.
>
> There through eternal boundless days,
> When nature's wheel no longer rolls,
> How shall I love, adore, and praise,
> This good Samaritan to souls![5]

But here's the problem. While it might make a great hymn, such an interpretation completely ignores the context in Luke's Gospel. A lawyer asked Jesus, "Who is my neighbor?" It doesn't make sense that he would respond by telling a story about the history of redemption. And when he was finished with the story, Jesus asked, "Which of these three do you think was a neighbor to the man who fell into the hands of the robbers?" So clearly Jesus wasn't thinking about the redemption of mankind here.

But Augustine was not troubled by the context. Neither was Origen or Newton. To them, there's validity in all three levels—the physical, the psychic, and the mystic. It's just a question of how deep your understanding of the passage is. So to them, you need not deny the literal or moral aspects of the story in order to interpret it allegorically.

Of course, Augustine's allegorical interpretation assumes that the ultimate message of the parable was something beyond the understanding of those who first heard it. No one in the days of Jesus would have associated the Apostle Paul with the innkeeper! Besides, the story of redemption requires a crucifixion, a resurrection, and an ascension into heaven, events that had not yet happened.

John Calvin, who opposed much of the rampant allegoricalism of his day, wrote,

> I acknowledge that I have no liking for [this type of] interpretation. We ought to have a deeper reverence for Scripture than to reckon ourselves at liberty to disguise its natural meaning. And, indeed, anyone may see that the curiosity of certain men has led them to contrive these speculations, contrary to the intention of Christ.[6]

Interpretive Influences

It's only natural that people would interpret any parable in light of their own world-view, their desires and experiences. Harry Emerson Fosdick (1878-1969) serves as an example. Fosdick was a central figure in the Fundamentalist-Modernist controversy back in the 1920s and 1930s. He was deeply committed to social justice. His commitment to social justice (sometimes called the "social gospel"), became the lens through which he interpreted the Parable of the Good Samaritan.

To Fosdick, the parable demonstrates different philosophies that people have towards their physical possessions. Furthermore, these philosophies are seen in us as individuals and even in the nations of the world.[7] And so, the attitude of the robbers in the parable is "What's yours is mine and I'll take it." That is, I am entitled to whatever I can get out of life, and by whatever means is necessary to acquire it. And again, in Fosdick's view, this could apply to nations as well as individuals. History is filled with acts of aggression by the strong against the weak.

The second attitude about possessions is expressed by the statement, "What's mine is mine and I'll keep it." The priest and the Levite who passed by on the far side of the road represented this view. They simply didn't want to get involved. They were isolationist in their approach. Their attitude was, "If you don't bother me then I won't bother you. I'll make as much money as I can, but don't expect much in terms of charity from me. The plight of the poor is the problem of the poor."

In Fosdick's view, this attitude is even worse than that of the robbers. Yes, the robbers stole from the man and left him for dead. But then, that's exactly what we would expect them to do. We would expect more from the priest and the Levite, however. Instead, these upstanding guardians of religion and morals were absolutely useless in the face of genuine need. To see suffering, have the ability to ease it and yet do nothing about it, makes you complicit in the need. You cannot simply say, "It's not my problem" when you have the ability to provide some assistance. That's why the priest and the Levite come off even worse than the robbers do in this parable. But more on this later.

And, of course, a third possible attitude about possessions is found in the expression, "What's mine is yours and I'll share it." This is the attitude of the Good Samaritan, who demonstrates pity by binding up the victim's wounds with oil and wine, placing him upon his own donkey, taking him to an inn, and paying for the lodging out of his own pocket. "What's mine is yours and I'll share it" is the attitude of benevolence. It's the attitude of Christ himself.

Now that's a catchy three-point outline that you can remember! "What's yours is mine and I'll take it; What's mine is mine and I'll keep it; What's mine is yours and I'll share it." But please understand that such an outline, while based on the text, flows out of the social context and concern of the interpreter, in this case Harry Emerson Fosdick.

In the same way, the hymn by John Newton given earlier came out of his life experience. You may recall that Newton was a slave trader before becoming a Christian. He was writing out of his own experience when he wrote:

> O! I remember well the day,
> When sorely wounded, nearly slain;
> Like that poor man I bleeding lay,
> And groaned for help, but groaned in vain.

As he interpreted the parable, he strongly identified with the man who fell among the robbers. He was writing about himself. But then, that's one of the things that makes the Bible so powerful. It speaks to each of us in the area of our own need.

Discussion

1. Can you recall where you were when you were first exposed to the story of the Good Samaritan? Church? Sunday School? Summer camp? Someplace else?
2. Is there an institution or organization named "Good Samaritan" where you live?
3. How ethnically and religiously diverse was your neighborhood while growing up? How aware were you of these differences at the time? Did it matter to you?

4. How have your attitudes about race and religion changed over the years? What social and spiritual factors do you attribute to these changes?
5. When it comes to interpreting and applying scripture, have most of the sermons that you've heard follow a *physical, psychic,* or *mystical* approach? Can you think of any recent examples?
6. In what ways have your past experiences and upbringing influenced how you approach the Bible? (Factors may include such things as: being raised in a Christian home, a history of substance abuse, domestic violence, financial affluence or poverty, being a "straight A" student, being a star athlete, etc.)

Chapter 3

The Attorney and His Agenda

(Luke 10:25-29)

As Luke sets the stage for the Parable of the Good Samaritan, he lays a foundation that's very similar to another episode found in both Matthew and Mark. In fact, they're so similar that some scholars believe they refer to one and the same incident. So, it might be helpful to consider Matthew 22:34-40 as we begin.

> Hearing that Jesus had silenced the Sadducees, the Pharisees got together. One of them, an expert in the law, tested him with this question: "Teacher, which is the greatest commandment in the Law?" Jesus replied: "'Love the Lord your God with all your heart and with all your soul and with all your mind.' This is the first and greatest commandment. And the second is like it: 'Love your neighbor as yourself.' All the Law and the Prophets hang on these two commandments." (Matthew 22:34-40)

The parallel passage in Mark 12:28-32 is substantially the same. As we compare Matthew and Mark with the Luke's preface to the Parable of the Good Samaritan, we notice that there are some similarities, as well as some differences.

In all three gospels it is a lawyer who approaches Jesus and asks a question. But while the answer is identical in all three cases, the question that the lawyer asks is not. In Matthew the question is phrased "Which is the greatest commandment in the law?" (Matthew 22:36) and in Mark it's recorded as "Of all of the commandments, which is the most important?" (Mark 12:28) In Luke, however, the question is very different: "What must I do to inherit eternal life?" (Luke 10:25) In any case, the answer is the same in all three instances. All three quote the Old Testament about loving God with all that is within you and loving your neighbor as you love yourself.

But there are some important differences in what we read in Matthew and Mark versus what Luke records for us. For one thing, in Luke Jesus turns the question back to the lawyer, asking "What is written in the law? How do you read it?" (Luke 10:26) and it's the lawyer who answers the question. In Matthew and Mark, however, Jesus answers the question directly.

There are other differences as well. Luke positions this encounter before Jesus enters Jerusalem on Palm Sunday, while Matthew and Mark place it on the Tuesday after Palm Sunday. What's more, the attitude of the lawyer seems to be somewhat neutral as Mark tells the story, while in Matthew and Luke the lawyer appears to be adversarial to Jesus.

Of course, the biggest difference between the three accounts is that only Luke uses this encounter between the lawyer and Jesus as a springboard for the Parable of the Good Samaritan. This parable won't be found in Matthew or in Mark, and certainly not in John, who is silent about the whole issue.

So did Matthew and Mark write about the same encounter that Luke did, or did they write about two separate events? I believe the "two event" theory fits the synoptic gospel narratives best for three reasons. First, both of the questions that were asked are the kind commonly raised at the time in Israel. To ask "Which of the commandments is most important?" or "How can I inherit eternal life?" is exactly the kind of issue that religious leaders often debated in the days of Jesus. So, it is not too much of a stretch to assume that with so many people asking Jesus these kinds of questions, two of them might be lawyers.

Second, the details about these two encounters seem too different to be easily harmonized—details about the setting, the questions asked, who gave the answer, and so forth. Therefore, there doesn't appear to be any "literary dependence" required here.

Finally, the lawyer's question in Luke serves as an appropriate introduction to the parable that follows. As we'll soon see, the question and the parable are presented as a unified event, occurring at the same time.

The Setting

We now turn our attention to how Luke sets the stage for the parable.

> On one occasion an expert in the law stood up to test Jesus. "Teacher," he asked, "what must I do to inherit eternal life?" "What is written in the Law?" he replied. "How do you read it?" He answered: "'Love the Lord your God with all your heart and with all your soul and with

all your strength and with all your mind'; and, 'Love your neighbor as yourself.'" "You have answered correctly," Jesus replied. "Do this and you will live." But he wanted to justify himself, so he asked Jesus, "And who is my neighbor?" (Luke 10:25-29)

The passage begins "On one occasion" in the New International Version. The New Revised Standard Version, however, begins this section differently. It starts with the words "Just then," suggesting that this episode takes place at the *same time and place* as the episode that Luke positions immediately before it—that is, when Jesus, full of the Holy Spirit, praises God the Father for hiding spiritual truths from the wise and learned, while revealing them to little children. And then, turning to his disciples privately, Jesus blesses them, saying, "Blessed are the eyes that see what you see. For I tell you that many prophets and kings wanted to see what you see but did not see it, and to hear what you hear but did not hear it." (Luke 10:23-24) At this juncture we are immediately introduced to the lawyer (i.e. "just then").

The New International Version unfortunately translates the Greek words *kai idou* as "on one occasion," implying that Jesus' encounter with the lawyer took place at *another time and place* than the previous blessing of his disciples. But nowhere else in the Gospel of Luke do the words *kai idou* introduce a narrative that is disconnected from what immediately precedes it, so there seems to be little reason for making an exception here.

The Greek words *kai idou* simply mean "and look" or "behold." The word *eidon* (from which *idou* comes) implies that the "looking" here is with a view to perceiving whatever it is that you're looking at.[1] In essence, Luke begins this section by telling his readers, "Pay attention to what's about to happen! Look and understand!" As

Luke crafts his gospel story of Jesus, he uses these two words to warn us not to be like the so-called "wise and learned" people in the preceding passage—those who heard everything that Jesus had to say, but who didn't understand a word of it.

The Lawyer

So "just then" a lawyer stands up to test Jesus. A lawyer, of course, is an expert in the law. Luke does not call him a scribe, although many lawyers were, in fact, scribes. Instead, he's called a *nomikos*, or someone who is concentrates on the law. In other words, his life's pursuit focuses primarily on the first five books of Moses in the Old Testament. In addition, as a legal expert he is also concerned with how the Law of Moses is to be applied to his present day. Now, the law can be a very complex and confusing thing—not just to understand what it says, but particularly its meaning and application.

His question will pertain to eternal life, something that ought to concern everyone. The problem is that Moses, the one who brought the law, didn't have much to say about a life beyond this one. The prophets certainly did, but not Moses. This distinction is one of the major dividing points between the Sadducees and the Pharisees. The Sadducees only accepted the five books of Moses as inspired canon. Since those books are silent about life after death, the Sadducees denied the resurrection. The Pharisees, who accepted the Prophets as a part of their Bibles, also accepted the concept of life after death. So perhaps the lawyer's question is not simply about attaining eternal life. Perhaps it's also about whether or not *all* 39 books of the Old Testament are truly God's word.

Notice also that the lawyer stands up to ask Jesus his question. The implication, of course, is that everyone else is seated. The rabbis used to stand up to honor the reading of scripture and then sit down to expound upon it. It may be that Jesus had been teaching his disciples privately, yet formally at the time the lawyer asked his question.

Luke 10:25 says he stands up "to test" Jesus. While the words "to test" suggest an antagonistic attitude, they doesn't necessarily require one, so this phrase is somewhat ambiguous. When a teacher gives his students a test, it's not because he's angry at them or trying to embarrass them. And it's certainly not because he sees his students as his adversaries! It's because he wants to discover what they know, so that he can give them an appropriate grade. "To test," then, might simply imply that some sort of an evaluation is about to take place. For a student, it might even be offered as an incentive to study!

But still, who is this lawyer that he would publicly test Jesus, even if it is just to evaluate him? It takes a certain amount of arrogance to do what he has done. Had he gone to Jesus in private, like Nicodemus did (John 3:2), that would have been one thing. However, to give Jesus a public "pop quiz" on such an important issue makes it look like he was trying to entrap him. That's why most commentators believe that this question was designed to embarrass Jesus, or to discredit him in a public way. In addition, this interpretation is also in keeping with the way in which Luke uses the phrase "to test" elsewhere in his gospel account. In the Gospel of Luke, "to test" or "to tempt" is always seen in an adversarial light. There's no reason to believe it's any different in this case.

The Question

"Teacher," he asked, "what must I do to inherit eternal life?" (Luke 10:25) Calling Jesus a teacher is appropriate. Jesus was often called a teacher. It was a noble and respected title. But let's analyze the question. "What must I do to inherit eternal life?"

The lawyer makes the assumption that eternal life is something that a person can earn ("what must I *do*"). And yet he also says that he wants to *inherit* it. His question contradicts itself. It's like asking how much of a product you have to buy before you're eligible to receive a free gift. If you have to buy something first, then the gift isn't really free. Even those who win the lottery have to buy a ticket.

Generally when you inherit something, it's because the person who originally owned it has died and wanted you to have it. (Hebrews 9:16-17) Sometimes there are conditions attached to it, but usually not. Normally if you inherit something, the main requirement is that you're willing to receive it. By the way, that's what grace is all about. Grace is a free gift. But still, any gift must be received to be enjoyed. (2 Corinthians 6:1)

This lawyer, however, isn't thinking about grace. He's thinking about doing something that will merit God's attention, or perhaps even doing something that would put God in his debt. In that regard, perhaps he isn't so different from the Rich Young Ruler who later came to Jesus asking the very same question: "What must I do to inherit eternal life?" (Luke 18:18) We get the impression that both of these two people—the lawyer and the Rich Young Ruler—felt that eternal life was something that could be negotiated.

It's easy to see how they could feel that way. They were both in positions of privilege and status. They were both in the upper levels of society where anything they could possibly want could be had for the right price. Both knew how to negotiate for things. So we can well understand why the question "what must I do?" would be asked.[2]

Instead of answering the question directly, Jesus turns it back onto the questioner. He is speaking with a lawyer, so Jesus starts with the law. He asks "What is written in the law? How do you read it?" (Luke 10:26) Literally, the Greek text asks "What is your knowledge of the law?" In essence, Jesus is asking this lawyer for a summation of everything that the law teaches on the subject. A lawyer in a courtroom will usually make a closing argument, where he summarizes all of the evidence and testimony that have been given in such a way that he proves his case. That's exactly what Jesus is asking the lawyer to do here.

Incidentally, as R. C. H. Lenski observes, "The psychology is simply perfect."[3] The lawyer may well have asked the question from an adversarial position, but Jesus doesn't get defensive. Instead, he respects the man's legal training and his apparent commitment to the law, a commitment that Jesus also shares. Jesus invites the lawyer to cooperate with him in answering the question, without implying that he recognizes any possible antagonism between the two of them. Jesus also does not criticize the lawyer for the way in which the question was asked or even for interrupting him as he spoke privately with his disciples. What would Jesus have to gain by antagonizing this lawyer?

The Answer: Love God First

We don't know where this lawyer received his legal training, but his answer is theologically sound. The lawyer thinks immediately of the *shema,* which is one of the pinnacles of the Old Testament. The word *shema* is Hebrew for "to hear." It is the first word of a simple statement of faith that serves as the centerpiece of morning and evening Jewish prayer services, encapsulating the essence of Israel's monotheistic faith: "Hear, O Israel: The Lord our God, the Lord is one." (Deuteronomy 6:4) Because there is only one God, he becomes the foundation for everything that we do. The lawyer then recalls our response to such a statement of faith: "Love the Lord your God with all your heart and with all your soul and with all your strength." (Deuteronomy 6:5)

We're struck by how holistic our love for God must be. In essence, the Scripture calls upon us to love God with everything that is within us.[4] Love him with *all of your heart*—that is, with all of your emotions. The heart is the center of a person's inner being. It's who you are at your inner core. And love him with *all of your soul*— that is, with all of your conscious life. In all your waking moments you are aware of God. God is as close as the air you breathe. Next, love him with *all of your strength*—love him with all of your actions, even down to the motivation behind those actions.

But the lawyer isn't finished. He adds something to the *shema,* a fourth dimension to our love for God: "Love God with *all your mind*" he says. (Luke 10:27) Incidentally, when Jesus quotes the *shema* in Mark 12:30 and Matthew 22:37, he also includes the mind. The word used for "mind" here is not the common word *nous.* Instead, the word is *dianoia,* which refers to deep and discerning thought. Literally, it means "to think something through."[5] In other words, our love for God is worthy of the deepest and most thorough of our thoughts.

The Answer: Love Your Neighbor Also

The lawyer is not yet finished. He adds to his answer an important social dimension. Quoting a portion of Leviticus 19:18 he says, "Love your neighbor as yourself." Perhaps he said more than he knew, or at least, more than he was willing to admit. The context in Leviticus is that of judging with justice. That is, we are not to show deference to the rich and powerful over the poor and downtrodden. What's more, we are not to slander our neighbor, either. To the Lord, gossiping or telling embellished stories about your neighbor is a form of injustice, because your neighbor generally has no chance to defend himself against your allegations or to tell his side of the story.

George A. F. Knight observes that the phrase "love your neighbor as yourself" is really a rather misleading translation because it assumes that how you view yourself becomes the standard for how you ought to treat other people. If that's the case, then we might conclude that if a person suffers from low self-esteem it gives him license to devalue others as well. Knight asserts that a better translation is to "love your neighbor as a man like yourself."[6] In other words, your neighbor is just like you. He (or she) has feelings just like you do. He has hopes and dreams, fears and aspirations, just like you do. Yes, he is a sinner, just like you are, but he also has a deep longing to be valued and loved, just like you do. In short, just about everything that you would hope for yourself in life, your neighbor also wants to experience. So when you treat your neighbor with less than those ideals in mind, you are doing a disservice to him.

"Loving yourself" is often thought of as looking after your own self-interests. That is, to love yourself means that you place a high value and priority on yourself. But when you make your own personal interests the standard for how you treat others, it becomes a form of idolatry because you've made yourself the focal point of your ethics. A better understanding of loving yourself is to have the ability to see yourself as God sees you.

The words of Leviticus 19:18 that the lawyer quoted go beyond the so-called "Golden Rule," because most of us would like to be treated generously.[7] However, Christ did not seek to be treated generously. Nor did he demand the respect he so richly deserved as God's son. Rather, he laid aside his own personal interests to redeem us all. The Apostle Paul writes in Philippians 2:5-8, "Your attitude should be the same as that of Christ Jesus:

> Who, being in very nature God,
> did not consider equality with God something
> to be used to his own advantage;
> rather, he made himself nothing
> by taking the very nature of a servant,
> being made in human likeness.
> And being found in appearance as a man,
> he humbled himself
> by becoming obedient to death—
> even death on a cross!"

In Romans 15:3 Paul writes, "For even Christ did not please himself but, as it is written: 'The insults of those who insult you have fallen on me.'"

So, when the Scripture says that you are to love your neighbor as you love yourself, it reaches far beyond whatever you might desire for your own benefit. In essence, it values each person as a unique creation in the eyes of God, created in his image and perhaps more like you than you might want to admit.[8] And just as you might deny yourself of something that you desire because there's a long-term benefit for you to do so, so in the same way (if we are to promote our neighbor's best interest) it may require a sacrifice.

To love your neighbor as yourself, therefore, is not about doing little favors on occasion for him whenever it's convenient for you. It's about seeking his best interest, knowing that what benefits him will eventually benefit you as well, and bring glory to God.[9]

So the lawyer asked Jesus what he had to do to inherit eternal life and in return, Jesus asked him about what the law said. The lawyer said we must love God with everything that is within us and to love our neighbor in much the same way. Jesus couldn't find any fault in that answer. So he said, "You have answered correctly. Do this and you will live." (Luke 10:28) The verb is in the present imperative tense. In other words, "Keep on doing this. This is not something that you do once and for all; it is a continuing obligation."

What's Wrong?

Again we note that Jesus offers no criticism for the lawyer's answer. The lawyer gave a good, solid and Biblical response. What's more, Jesus agreed with him. So what's wrong with this conversation?

Fred Craddock notes several errors on the part of the lawyer.[10] First, the lawyer has asked a question for the purpose of gaining an advantage over another person. Remember, the lawyer sought to "test" Jesus, to embarrass him publicly. The irony should not be overlooked. The lawyer gives the right answer about loving other people, but the way in which he asks his question fails to display a loving spirit. He speaks all the right words, but his behavior is lacking.

Neighbors and Ne'er-Do-Wells

In addition, he has no desire or commitment to act upon the answer to his question. He asked, "What must I do?" without any intention of actually *doing* anything. Not only is his behavior lacking, but so is his attitude.

Students studying to become professional counselors are often advised, "If you don't want to know the answer to a question, don't ask it." It is sound advice. It serves little purpose to delve into areas in which you're not able or willing to provide any practical assistance. The lawyer asks a question about what he needs to do, but he has no intention of actually following through on anything.

And finally, he seems to assume that eternal life comes as a result of giving the correct answers to theological questions. But, as Professor Craddock observes, "Having the right answer does not mean one knows God. Students can make a four-point in Bible and miss the point. Jesus did not say to the lawyer, 'Great answer! You are my best pupil!' Rather, Jesus said, 'Go and do.'"[11]

Pressing a bit further, we can't help but to wonder if Jesus' answer wasn't also designed to reveal how impossible it is to keep all of the law's demands. After all, who in their own strength can love God as fully as the law requires, or to love a neighbor in the same way? Later, the Apostle Paul will summarize the impossibility of perfectly keeping the law by saying, "I found that the very commandment that was intended to bring life actually brought death." (Romans 7:10) The end result is that "by the works of the law no one will be justified." (Galatians 2:16) In short, apart from an act of God's mercy and grace, no one can ever hope for eternal life. Sadly, as Karl Barth asserts, "The lawyer does not know that only by mercy can he live and inherit eternal life. He does not want to live by mercy. He does not even know what mercy is."[12] What the lawyer wants is a checklist of what he needs to do in order to be assured of eternal life. He's confident in his own righteousness, so he says "Just tell me what I need to do and I'll get it done," without expecting much inconvenience.

Trying to Save Face

The last verse in this section is the most troubling verse of all—not in terms of understanding what it says, but in terms of what was really going on inside of the lawyer's heart. "But he wanted to justify himself, so he asked Jesus, 'And who is my neighbor?'" (Luke 10:29) This final question is the reason Jesus told the parable that follows, so it's good that he asked it. But look at what it reveals about the lawyer's heart.

"He wanted to justify himself." The context shows that this lawyer isn't thinking about being justified in the sight of God. Rather, he wants to justify his own actions. He has stood up publicly, trying to embarrass Jesus. Still, Jesus has interacted with him in such a way as to place them both on the same side. After all, they agreed with each other. They both said we need to love God and to love other people.

Perhaps the lawyer is now embarrassed by Jesus' agreement with him. After all, he stood up, posed a question and then answered it himself rather simply and succinctly. If the answer was all that simple, then why did he ask the question in the first place? Perhaps the lawyer feels foolish for having made a public spectacle of himself.

So the problem the lawyer now faces is this: "How can I get out of this awkward and embarrassing situation, given the fact that Jesus has revealed my true motivation?" He decides to ask another question as if to say, "Jesus, this isn't nearly as simple as you seem to think it is. So answer me this: 'Who is my neighbor?'"

To get the full impact of such a question, we need to remember the social milieu in which it was asked. To most Jews, a neighbor would, at the very least, be another Jew—but certainly it would not extend to a Samaritan or to a Gentile. In fact, some of the rabbis even taught that if you were to come across a Gentile woman who was in labor and in the process of giving birth, that it would be illegal to help her deliver her child, because it would bring another Gentile into the world.[13] Reflecting this attitude, Jonathan Swift put their sentiment to poetry when he sarcastically wrote:

> We are God's chosen few;
> All others will be damned.
> There is no room for you;
> We can't have heaven crammed![14]

But interestingly enough, their concept of neighborliness could even be construed as being narrower than that. At one point the Jewish leaders sent their temple police out to arrest Jesus. After listening to what Jesus was teaching, however, the police noticed that the crowd was divided as to who Jesus was. So they came back empty handed. When asked why they didn't arrest Jesus, they answered, "No one ever spoke the way this man does." (John 7:46)

The Pharisees were angry at their answer. "You mean he has deceived you also?" the Pharisees retorted. "Have any of the rulers or of the Pharisees believed in him? No! But this mob that knows nothing of the law—there is a curse on them." (John 7:47-49) Notice that the crowd—a crowd that was composed of Jews—was called "cursed" by the Pharisees. The implication, of course, is that these Jewish leaders weren't even convinced that some of their *own* number were really legitimate.

So, who is my neighbor? In short, we might surmise that your neighbor is only someone who is "one of us," but we can't be sure of *every* one of us! At the root of the Greek word for "neighbor" is the word for "near." But is a neighbor only someone who lives near to you? In Hebrew, a neighbor is generally thought of as someone with whom you have some form of association. Within a Hebrew context, that would mean fellow Jews, but certainly not Romans, Greeks or Assyrians. But narrowing it down even further, we might ask "Does being a neighbor imply an existing relationship and the sharing of common values and interests? Or can a person be a total stranger to you and yet still be considered your neighbor?"

The next chapter focuses on the amazing story that Jesus tells in answer to the question, "Who is my neighbor?"

Discussion

1. If someone were to ask you, "What's the most important thing that the Bible teaches," how would you answer?
2. Lawyers were highly respected in Jesus' day. What kind of a reputation do lawyers have today? Is that reputation deserved? Do you know any lawyers personally?
3. Think back to the last presidential press conference that you saw on television. How many of the questions had a bias or agenda attached to them? What do the questions that are asked tell us about those who ask them?
4. Can you recall an instance where someone was left an inheritance, but had to do something in order to qualify for it?
5. When it comes to loving God with all of your *heart, soul, strength,* and *mind,* which of these four aspects presents the greatest challenge for you?

6. Do you agree or disagree with the author's assertion that making yourself the standard for how you treat others can become a form of idolatry? Why or why not? If you yourself are not the best standard, then who or what is?
7. Fred Craddock says that the lawyer never had any intention of actually doing anything when he asked, "What must I do to inherit eternal life?" Yet, the author suggests that he wanted a checklist—"Just tell me what to do and I'll get it done." Do you find that there's often a conflict between what people *say* and what they're actually willing to *do*? Are you more of a talker or a doer?
8. Can you think of a time when you (or someone else) embarrassed themselves in public? What attempts were made to resolve the situation?
9. How inclusive is your church when it comes to associating with other churches? What factors do you think separate churches the most? (Examples might include: doctrine, music, style of worship, social involvement, the kind of ministry performed, etc.)

Chapter 4
Crime and Compassion
(Luke 10:30-35)

Before we delve into the Parable of the Good Samaritan itself, two important observations are in order.

Hypothetical, Not Historical

First, we must remember that this story, like all parables, is hypothetical and not historical. In other words, this is a story that originated in the mind of Jesus. He created it. He was not talking about an actual event.[1]

This is important to remember because while we are naturally curious about what prompted the characters to do what they did, we must be careful not to read too much into the story. For example, in this parable a priest and a Levite will come across a man who has fallen among robbers. Both will pass by on the other side of the road. As we listen to the story, we can't help but to wonder what their motivations were for not wanting to get involved. Perhaps they were in a hurry, or they didn't want to get their hands dirty.

Or perhaps they were even concerned about making themselves ceremonially unclean, rendering them useless for their ministry in the temple. Jesus, however, made no such speculation in the telling of this story. He didn't explore their motives, whether they were selfish or noble. Since Jesus didn't speculate on the reasoning behind the action of the priest and the Levite, we must be careful about placing too much importance on it.

However, two opposing views have been suggested regarding the characters' motivation. The first view is that motivation is simply not an important issue in this parable. If the attitudes behind the characters' actions were important, Jesus would have said so. Since he didn't, then speculating about attitudes might cause us to become distracted by things that Jesus didn't consider important enough to mention. In other words, may find ourselves majoring on minors, walking down the wrong path of interpretation, and drawing moral and theological conclusions based on what Jesus didn't say.

In contrast, the other view assumes that Jesus fully expected us to ponder what prompted the characters' behavior in his stories. It's human nature to do so. We must remember that one of the great strengths of any parable is its ability to drawn the listener into it. There is an emotive quality in every parable, especially this one. So there's a natural tendency for us to question why the man who fell among robbers was traveling this dangerous road alone, why the priest and Levite passed by on the other side, or even what the Samaritan's wife thought when she found out her husband had spent two denarii on a total stranger (assuming the Samaritan was married, of course). Questions such as these bring the story to life.

To refuse to consider the motivation behind the character's actions can render the story cold and sterile, robbing it of much of its power. So a balance needs to be maintained. While some speculation is natural, we must tread lightly, being careful not to read too much into the parable that simply isn't there. Everything that is necessary for understanding the parable's message is within the parable itself. Understanding the cultural setting and context is vital, of course, but the key elements stand *within* the parable, not apart from it.

So we conclude that the Parable of the Good Samaritan is not primarily a parable about a person's attitude. It's a parable about a person's conduct. And when it is all over, Jesus will conclude by saying, "Go and do likewise." (Luke 10:37) He will not say, "Go and work on your attitude!" Still, that's not to say that our attitude is unimportant. It does say, however, that this parable does not address our attitude as a major issue. There are other passages in the Bible that address the importance of having a good attitude, but not this one.[2]

Now, for those who use an allegorical approach in interpreting this parable, speculating about things absent from the text poses no problem at all. In an allegory, every detail points to something else entirely. You'll recall that Augustine found the history of redemption outlined in this parable. Still, such an interpretation goes way beyond the immediate context. While Jesus did tell some allegorical parables, he never interpreted this one allegorically, nor did any of the apostles. So we shouldn't either.

Warning!

The second observation before we enter into the text comes in the form of a warning. When approaching well-known stories such as this, we should "Read it again for the first time." In 1990 a new commercial was aired on television advertising Kellogg's Corn

Flakes®. Corn Flakes had been around for a long time. In fact, many adults had eaten Corn Flakes as children. The makers of Corn Flakes wanted to reintroduce the adult market to this breakfast cereal. Since most people already knew what Corn Flakes tasted like, they advertised "Taste them again for the first time." In other words, put aside your preconceived notions and experience Corn Flakes in a new and fresh way.³

> When approaching well-known stories such as this, we should "Read it again for the first time."

Are you already familiar with the Parable of the Good Samaritan? "Read it again for the first time." This is especially good advice for Bible preachers and teachers. There's a great temptation as we prepare a Bible study or sermon on this parable not to allow ourselves the minute and a half it takes to actually read it. As a result, our preconceived notions are reinforced, creativity is stifled, and ultimately God's Holy Spirit is not allowed to work with His Word in new and fresh ways.

So, let's read this story again for the first time. Let's try to put aside all of our preconceived notions and hear it as if we were in the audience at the precise moment this story was first told.

The Parable

There's a bit of tension in the air. A lawyer stands up and tries to publicly embarrass Jesus. People are seated all around, wondering how Jesus is going to react. But without any sign of animosity, Jesus agrees with everything that the lawyer says. The greatest commandments are to love God and to love your neighbor. "And who is my neighbor?" the lawyer asks. So Jesus begins his story:

> A man was going down from Jerusalem to Jericho, when he was attacked by robbers. They stripped him of his clothes, beat him and went away, leaving him half dead. A priest happened to be going down the same road, and when he saw the man, he passed by on the other side. So too, a Levite, when he came to the place and saw him, passed by on the other side. But a Samaritan, as he traveled, came where the man was; and when he saw him, he took pity on him. (Luke 10:30-33)

The first thing we note is that a man is traveling down from Jerusalem to Jericho. Those who originally heard this story understood exactly what that meant. They knew that stretch of highway. It was a dangerous road about 20 miles long. Since Jerusalem was high atop Mount Zion, it meant a drop of nearly 3,600 feet. So, Jesus was absolutely right when he said that the man was traveling *down* from Jerusalem to Jericho. Topographically speaking, everyone travels *down* when leaving Jerusalem.

Because of the steep descent, the road was filled with switchbacks, cutting back and forth across the mountainside. Any one of these switchbacks was a potential a hiding place for thieves. This was *not* a safe road to travel! Pompey, the Roman military and political leader, was forced to "wipe out strongholds of brigands near Jericho" roughly forty years before Jesus was born. Nearly 500 years later, Jerome, an early Christian apologist and translator of the Bible into Latin, called this piece of highway "The Bloody Way" because so many robberies were still taking place along it.[4] Later, during the Crusades, a small fort was built at the halfway point between Jerusalem and Jericho to protect pilgrims as they traveled the road.[5] Today the road still exists, although it is traveled primarily by tourists. It is dry, dusty, and inhospitable. The road has been superseded by Highway 1, a paved four-lane national highway, 58 miles long, linking Jerusalem with Tel Aviv by way of Jericho.

But who is this man who's traveling alone along this dangerous highway? We simply don't know. Remember, this story is a piece of fiction, designed to teach us a truth beyond the story itself. All we know is what Jesus tells us. We must assume that if his identity was important, we would have been told so. The audience to whom Jesus was speaking, however, would certainly assume that the traveler was like themselves—Jewish. Still, we must be cautious at this point because they were in an ethnically diverse region. In any event, the man "was attacked by robbers. They stripped him of his clothes, beat him and went away, leaving him half dead." (Luke 10:30)

No less than William Barclay, the great Scottish pastor and theologian, speculated that this man was "obviously a reckless and foolhardy character" who "had no one but himself to blame for the plight in which he found himself."[6] After all, everyone knew how dangerous that road was. That's why people typically traveled in groups along that road, especially if they were carrying anything of value on their person. Such speculation does a disservice to this parable, however. This parable is not ultimately about the man who fell among robbers. To speculate about his character or about whether he deserved to be robbed is a diversion from the main point of the story. Furthermore, we gain little understanding of what it means to be a neighbor by blaming the victim.[7]

The robbers take absolutely everything of value that this man has, even down to his very clothing. They strip him and beat him, leaving him *half dead*. The Greek word is *hēmithanē* and this is the only place in the New Testament where it appears. It's a compound word that literally means to be "halfway to death." In other words, this man's life was in the process of ebbing away from him. Such a condition is entirely consistent with being savagely beaten. In our imagination we can picture him lying curled on the ground with his life's blood draining from him.

A person who is "halfway to death" is weak, perhaps unconscious, and by all appearances has already died. But in any case, he is helpless and unless some intervention takes place, will most likely die "the rest of the way."

The Priest

Jesus continues with his story: "A priest happened to be going down the same road, and when he saw the man, he passed by on the other side." (Luke 10:31). Priests were tasked with ministry within the temple in Jerusalem. A rabbi would minister in local synagogues, but priests served in the temple. A major feature of their ministry was the offering of sacrifices, but they also pronounced blessings, arranged for temple music (both vocal and instrumental), blew trumpets on festive occasions, oversaw the temple treasury, and performed rites of purification.[8] If someone was declared to be "unclean", it required a trip to a priest to be purified. On at least two separate occasions after healing people of their leprosy, Jesus commanded them to go to the priests for ceremonial purification and certification. (Luke 5:14; 17:14)

Since priests were among the élite, upper class in Jewish society those who originally heard Jesus' parable would have naturally envisioned him riding an animal of some sort.[9] Without offering any elaboration or explanation, Jesus simply states that the priest was traveling down the same road, saw the half dead man, and passed by on the other side.

In the absence of any elaboration on Jesus' part, some Bible teachers defend the priest's action. They point out that, by all appearances, this man was dead. They quote the Old Testament law which says, "Whoever touches a human corpse will be unclean for seven days." (Numbers 19:11) The priest certainly couldn't perform his ministry in the temple if he were to become ceremonially unclean. Thus, some defenders of the priest argue that he was simply answering a higher calling when he passed by on the other side of the road.

Such a view might have some merit except as Jesus tells the story, the priest was traveling *down* the road, not *up* the road at the time. The direction is important. Remember, Jerusalem is located high atop Mount Zion. Everyone travels *down* from there. Since the priest was traveling *down,* he had to be traveling *away* from Jerusalem and towards Jericho. If he was expecting to perform some form of ministry in the temple he was going in the wrong direction!

In addition, if the natural assumption that the priest was riding an animal is correct, it only adds to his guilt. Had he been on foot he might have thought, "What good I can do out here in the middle of nowhere?" He had no cell phone with which to call 9-1-1 and no means of getting the half-dead man to a place where he could receive medical attention. Still, if he had an animal on which to ride, he could have at least transported the man. Defenders of the priest in this story, assuming him to be on foot, sometimes assert "Of course the Samaritan should have helped the man. He was the only one who was really in a position to do so." Yet as Jesus structures the story there is a presumption that *anyone* who was willing to help could have done so.[10]

A cultural expectation of helping strangers in this kind of situation also helps us to understand the priest's unwillingness to get involved.[11] Ben Sirach was a Jewish scribe who lived about 150 years before Christ. He authored *The Wisdom of Sirach* (also known as *Ecclesiasticus*) which, while not accepted into the Hebrew Bible, nevertheless serves as a dependable commentary of Jewish ethics of the period and as such is still widely studied today. In Sirach 12:1, 4-5a, 6-7 we read:

> If you do a good turn, know for whom you are doing it . . . Give to a devout man, but *do not go to the help of a sinner.* Do good to a humble man, but *give nothing to a godless one.* Refuse him bread, do not give him any, for he might become stronger than you are . . . For the Most High himself detests sinners and will repay the wicked with a vengeance. Give to a good man, but *do not go to the help of a sinner."*

In short, Ben Sirach counseled against helping someone who might be a sinner, for to do so would work against God's righteous purpose. By helping a sinner you'd only be strengthening evil in our world. The assumption of the day was that people get what they deserve in life.[12] If this man was robbed, stripped, beaten, and left for dead, they felt it was a good indication that he was a sinner. What better reason for the priest to simply chose to pass him by? Why promote unrighteousness?

Of course, Ben Sirach's view is incompatible with Christian ethics. The Apostle Paul writes,

> Do not repay anyone evil for evil. Be careful to do what is right in the eyes of everyone. If it is possible, as far as it depends on you, live at peace with everyone. Do not take revenge, my dear friends, but leave room for God's wrath, for it is written: "It is mine to avenge; I will repay," says the Lord. On the contrary: "If your enemy is hungry, feed him; if he is thirsty, give him something to drink. In doing this, you will heap burning coals on his head." *Do not be overcome by evil, but overcome evil with good.* (Romans 12:17-21, emphasis mine)

We must be careful, however, that we not allow our speculation about the priest's motivation to divert us too much from the main point of the story. Remember, Jesus neither defends nor condemns the priest. He merely states that he was traveling that same stretch of highway, that he saw the man who had been robbed, stripped, beaten and left half-dead, and that he passed by on the other side of the road. If we're going to "read this story again for the first time" we must, at least for the present, withhold judgment about this priest. Let's not jump to conclusions too soon, for the story is only half over.

The Levite

Jesus continues, "So too, a Levite, when he came to the place and saw him, passed by on the other side." (Luke 10:32) Levites, like priests, had a special role in temple ministry. They were descendants of Levi who assisted the priests in the performance of various sacrificial duties, although they were not authorized to perform the ritual of sacrifice itself. In addition, they were responsible for temple maintenance and would police the grounds to make sure everything was in order.[13]

Some have suggested that since the Levites supported the priesthood, they were of secondary importance. In addition, since there were more Levites than priests, the problem of becoming defiled by touching a dead body would be less acute for them. The priest in Jesus' parable couldn't very well become temporarily unclean by helping this wounded traveler, but the Levite was much more expendable. It would be much easier for a Levite to find a suitable replacement that it would be for a priest. Therefore, some argue that the Levite carried more responsibility to assist the wounded traveler than the priest did.

A close examination of Jesus' words, however, doesn't reveal any such "second class" spiritual status on the part of the Levites. They had their important and legitimate function, just as the priests had theirs. Still, while the Levites were in a lower economic and social class, it seems that Jesus groups the priest and the Levite together in this parable without much of a distinction between the two of them. In other words, they were both religious professionals who came across the same situation, responding in much the same way. There was a slight difference, however.

How close did these two professionals physically venture toward the half dead man? The priest "saw the man" and "passed by on the other side." In our imagination we can picture him reining his animal over and away from the man, without even dismounting. The Levite, on the other hand, could well have been on foot. He "came to the place" and saw the man, implying that perhaps he came closer him than the priest did. In any case, the end result was the same. They both passed by on the other side of the road.

Their action, then, is at the crux of the problem. The question that prompted this story was "Who is my neighbor?" Whatever being a good neighbor entails, we would hope that these two religious professionals would understand it and act upon it. But such is not the case.

End Stress: The Samaritan

At this point Jesus employs a dynamic called "The Rule of End Stress." The Rule of End Stress says that a parable generally builds in intensity, with a crescendo to the climax. The main thrust of the story usually appears at the end, often as a surprise. In other words, there's a twist at the end of the story where the moral can be found.

The first part of the story sets the stage for the critical issue, which comes at the close.[14] In this case, Jesus introduces a Samaritan who happens to be traveling that same dangerous stretch of highway.[15] We need to recall the social context here. Palestine was a racially mixed area. There were those of pure Jewish ancestry, but there were also Romans, Assyrians and remnants of the Canaanite population.

We must remember that when the area of Samaria fell to the Assyrians its leading Jewish citizens were exiled and dispersed all throughout the Assyrian Empire. People of mixed ancestry then began settling in the area, resulting in the remaining Jews intermarrying with these Gentile settlers. Their children were considered unclean "half-breeds" by most full-blooded Jews, who resided in the South.[16] The animosity between these two groups was heightened when the Southern Jews returned after the exile and started to rebuild the Jerusalem temple. The mixed-Jews from Samaria offered their assistance, but because of their mixed ancestry their assistance was rejected. As a result, many of them retaliated by trying to impede progress on the rebuilding of the temple. The Samaritans finally built their own temple up north on Mount Gerizim. Then it was time for "payback," as the full-blooded Jews from the south sought revenge by raiding the Samaritan temple and destroying it. Not many years before Jesus told this parable Samaritans had escalated things even further by returning to the Jerusalem temple, scattering human bones in the court, thus defiling it. There was clearly no love lost between the Jews and the Samaritans. The racial, cultural, social and spiritual animosity that existed in Jesus' day cannot be overlooked when interpreting this parable.

As Luke records Jesus' parable, the original Greek text shows the word "Samaritan" in the emphatic position. That is, it is the first word in the sentence, giving it special emphasis. Jesus does not say, "And then a third person came by, who happened to be a Samaritan." Instead, he literally says, "Samaritan journeying came upon him," emphasizing the word "Samaritan." It is no mere accident that Jesus chooses a Samaritan to come across this wounded traveler. In so doing, he selects a religious and social outsider—and a hated one at that.

When Jesus introduces a Samaritan into this story, we can't help but to wonder what must have been going through the lawyer's mind. If fine, upstanding religious professionals like priests and Levites pass by without harming this helpless man, what cruel act of barbarity might a Samaritan do to him? Remember, we want to "read this story again for the first time." The lawyer has no idea that the Samaritan is going to turn out to be the hero.[17]

And yet, utilizing the "Rule of End Stress," Jesus turns everything upside down: "But a Samaritan, as he traveled, came where the man was; and when he saw him, he took pity on him." (Luke 10:33) Far from kicking the man when he's down, this hated Samaritan is actually moved with pity towards him. And the word for pity here is the colorful Greek word *splanchnon,* which is often translated as "bowels," "inner organs," or "intestines." When the Samaritan came upon the wounded traveler, he was deeply moved within.

A Neighbor in Action

We now come to the critical juncture in the story. Remember that the question that prompted this parable was "Who is my neighbor?" As we read on we discover what being a neighbor entails.

> He went to him and bandaged his wounds, pouring on oil and wine. Then he put the man on his own donkey, brought him to an inn and took care of him. The next day he took out two denarii and gave them to the innkeeper. "Look after him," he said, "and when I return, I will reimburse you for any extra expense you may have." (Luke 10:34-35)

First, notice that "he went to him," which perhaps is the greatest aspect of what it means to be a neighbor. The priest only "saw the man" and the Levite "came to the place" where he was, but the Samaritan "went to him." There is no avoidance when it comes to being a neighbor. It's taking the initiative to be present when you could have gone in another direction.

He then bandaged his wounds, after pouring oil and wine on them. Oil and wine were considered to be medicinal in that day. Olive oil served to ease pain. Although the ancients were unaware of the antiseptic properties of wine, they nevertheless knew from experience that it aided in the healing process. These remedies were widely used among both Jews and Gentiles at the time.[18]

Since the lawyer who first heard this parable was well versed in Judaism, perhaps the image of oil and wine had a sacramental connotation as well. They were commonly used in temple worship. We also note that Jesus used the word "pour" (*epicheōn*) to describe how the oil and wine were applied. Libations were often offered in connection with sacrifices. The irony should not be missed. The priest and the Levite would have been very familiar with pouring oil and wine upon the altar as a part of their service in the temple. In the absence of any help on their part, however, the Samaritan's act of kindness assumes a sacramental role as he offers himself as a "living sacrifice." (Romans 12:1)[19]

Perhaps Jesus had hoped that the lawyer, picturing the imagery in his mind, would be reminded of God's words to Hosea, "For I desire mercy, not sacrifice, and acknowledgment of God rather than burnt offerings." (Hosea 6:6) Or perhaps these words from Micah were in the back of Jesus' mind:

> With what shall I come before the Lord
> and bow down before the exalted God?
> Shall I come before him with burnt offerings,
> with calves a year old?
> Will the Lord be pleased with thousands of rams,
> with ten thousand rivers of olive oil?
> Shall I offer my firstborn for my transgression,
> the fruit of my body for the sin of my soul?
> He has shown you, O mortal, what is good.
> *And what does the Lord require of you?*
> *To act justly and to love mercy*
> *and to walk humbly with your God.*
> (Micah 6:6-8, emphasis mine)

Both the priest and the Levite were well versed in the mechanics of temple worship, but it didn't affect their personal lives very well. They failed to do "what the Lord required." The Samaritan, although he was an outsider as far as temple worship in Jerusalem was concerned, understood mercy much better than the religious professionals did.

Continuing with the story, the Samaritan put him on his own animal. The very presence of an animal to ride hints at the Samaritan's economic status, since the poor rarely rode. Since the beaten traveler was "half dead" he was certainly unable to walk and probably would need assistance just staying on top of a donkey's back!

The Samaritan then brought the man to an inn, where he "took care of him." That is, he didn't just drop him off, hoping that someone else would assume responsibility for him. But the Samaritan evidently could not stay there for a prolonged period of time, so he continued his care by making arrangements with the innkeeper to nurse the traveler back to health. After all, the wounded man had been robbed and therefore had no money of his own. The Samaritan gave the innkeeper two denarii up front, saying "I will reimburse you for any extra expense you may have." (Luke 10:35) The word *I* is in an emphatic position. To paraphrase the Good Samaritan, "I myself will pay the bill, so don't trouble the injured man for payment."

These two denarii (small silver coins) represent two days' worth of wages for a common worker and would have paid for roughly two weeks of lodging.[20] If it is true that money is "coined life," then this act of neighborliness cost the Samaritan two days of his life. Sometimes there's a price to be paid for being neighborly.

This is where the story ends. Jesus leaves us in suspense. What's the point that he's trying to make? What conclusions should we draw on the basis of this parable? How should we apply it? What does it say about our own interpersonal relationships, racism, or even the relationships between nations?

Discussion

1. Most scholars believe the Parable of the Good Samaritan is a fictional story created by Jesus. A few, however, believe that Jesus referred to an actual event. Does it make a difference to you? Why or why not? What of the historicity of other Biblical

events, such as the crucifixion and resurrection of Christ? Explain your reasoning.
2. How important is a person's attitude when it comes to his or her behavior? Give an example of when you did the right thing, but had a bad attitude about it. (See Matthew 21:28-32)
3. Are there some dangerous areas where you live in which you might not want to venture out after dark? How would you characterize those people who do?
4. Have you ever been the victim of a robbery? How did your experience affect your attitude and/or behavior?
5. In contrast to the priest and the Levite, can you think of a religious professional (pastor, church staff member, etc.) who has been especially helpful to you in the past? Why did you think of him or her?
6. How are today's hitchhikers and beggars similar or different from those of Jesus' day? When you come across one, do you tend to help them on their terms? Do something else? Do nothing at all? What's your reasoning?
7. As far as the Jews were concerned, Samaritans were religious and social outcastes. Who are the "Samaritans" of today? Do you know a "Samaritan" personally?
8. Can you recall a time when someone you didn't especially like helped you out? Or when you assisted someone you were in conflict with? How did that action affect your relationship?
9. Time and resources don't allow us to help everyone all of the time. What criteria do you use in deciding when and when not to get involved? Do you tend to want to do things directly by yourself, or through organizations?

Chapter 5

The Answer and Some Applications

(Luke 10:36-37)

When we last left Jesus and the lawyer, Jesus had finished telling a story that we have come to call "The Parable of the Good Samaritan." The lawyer had stood up in order to embarrass Jesus by putting him to the test. "What must I do to inherit eternal life?" he asked. Jesus turned the question back onto the lawyer: "What is written in the law? How do you read it?" The lawyer then summed up the Old Testament law by saying we need to love God with everything that is within us and that we need to love our neighbor as we ourselves would like to be loved. Jesus agreed with the lawyer. "You have answered correctly" he said, "Do this and you will live." (Luke 10:25-28)

Of course, this wasn't the answer that the lawyer was looking for. But then, he wasn't looking for answers.

Imagine the scene. The lawyer had interrupted Jesus as he spoke with his disciples. As he stood there every eye was upon him. How could he extricate himself from this awkward situation? Thinking on his feet, he asked Jesus, "And who is my neighbor?"

A neighbor is often thought of as someone who lives in close proximity to you. But how close is close? Do your neighbors include people of different religions and ethnicities? If so, is there a legitimate double standard that should be used? Is there one standard of conduct as it relates to people who are like you (be it culturally, economically, politically, or spiritually), and yet another lower, standard that can be applied to everyone else?

In the parable it is a hated Samaritan who turns out to be the hero and not the religious professionals. It is the Samaritan who stops, who is filled with pity, who binds up the man's wounds with oil and wine, who puts him on his own animal, who pays for lodging at the inn, and who pledges future payment should it be required.

This, then, brings us to the critical juncture in the story. Back in verse 29 the lawyer had asked "Who is my neighbor?" But now, Jesus revises that question in a significant way. After telling the story he asks, "Which of these three do you think was a neighbor to the man who fell into the hands of robbers?" (Luke 10:36)

Who is a Neighbor?

The question is no longer "Who is *my* neighbor?" It is now "To whom am *I* a neighbor?" The distinction may seem slight, but it is quite significant. If the question remains "Who is my neighbor," then the natural assumption is that there are some people who are not my neighbors. If that's the case, I need to know where my responsibility to non-neighbors ends.

> The question is no longer "Who is *my* neighbor?" It is now "To whom am *I* a neighbor?"

Michael Lodahl is professor of theology and world religions at Point Loma Nazarene University in San Diego, California. He tells about a time when he was working on his Ph.D. about 20 years ago. He was at a prayer breakfast at the local Church of the Nazarene when he came across someone he had never met before. They introduced themselves and then started getting to know each other.

Lodahl asked if his new friend had been raised in a Nazarene Church. "No," he said, he was actually raised as a Quaker. One of Lodahl's classmates in school was a Quaker, so he said, "The Quakers have a lot of good folks." When his new friend heard that comment, he replied, "Yeah? Well, I left the Quaker church during the war in Vietnam."

After an uncomfortable pause, Lodahl said, "Oh really. Why was that?" It was at this point that the man started to share his deeper feelings. He said that the Quakers have always been pacifists. They didn't believe in war as a means of settling international differences, but whenever a war *did* break out, they have traditionally provided a lot of humanitarian aid to civilians displaced by the conflict. And then he said, "You know, they set up medical units during the war that helped the North Vietnamese." He was clearly upset that his church, in its attempt to alleviate human suffering, did not make a distinction between North and South Vietnamese. They sought to bring relief to *all* people, regardless of who they were.

In retrospect, Lodahl says he should have probably just remained silent and finished eating his breakfast. Instead he felt moved to ask one last question: "Well, Jesus did tell us to love our enemies, didn't he?" Without a moment's hesitation the man responded, "That's where I draw the line!"[1]

Acts of kindness to friends and allies is one thing, but where do you draw the line? For this man, helping the enemy, even if they were non-combatants like he was, was over the line. Certainly there must be a limit somewhere.

The lawyer's question reflects his reasoning: "I'm commanded to love my neighbor and I'm willing to do so. I just need to know where to draw the line. Is the person in the next town over my neighbor? How about in the next county or state? How about someone living in a foreign country? Or someone of a different race or religion? Where does it all end?"[2]

Or *does* it all end? The question is now, "To whom am *I* a neighbor?" Remember, Jesus asked, "which of the three was a neighbor?" Some translations render this verse, "which one *proved* himself to be a neighbor?" Neighborliness isn't something that originates outside of yourself. It starts within you. It must be demonstrated by you.

I Am Your Neighbor

The emphasis in this parable is on each and every one of us. I cannot define neighborliness by what I see in *you*. I must define it in terms of what *my own* behavior requires. You may be worthy or unworthy, likable or unlikable, rich or poor, American or foreign, friendly or unfriendly, Catholic or Protestant, Christian or non-Christian, it really doesn't matter. The way in which I treat you does not depend on who you are. It depends on who *I* am—my values and ultimately, my faith.

In Old English, a neighbor was someone who was "nigh." He was close by. That same idea is also suggested in Hebrew and especially in Greek. But Jesus turns it around. A neighbor isn't someone who happens to come near to you—as if it all depends upon what other people are doing. When Jesus asked "Which one was a neighbor," he was talking about a state of being. So, think of it like this: If I become a neighbor to everyone, then everyone becomes a neighbor to me. And what's more, there is no one who is not my neighbor. This then, means that I must take the initiative in being a good neighbor. The burden is upon *me* to draw near to others in a neighborly fashion—to *become* their neighbor—and not to merely pass by on the other side of the road as the priest and the Levite did.[3]

This is one of the reasons why interpreting this parable as an allegory doesn't fit very well. Beyond the fact that an allegorical interpretation completely ignores the story's context, it also tends to relieve the listener of any and all responsibility. As we've seen, Augustine saw the history of redemption in this story. In his view, the Good Samaritan typifies Jesus himself. But if Jesus is the Good Samaritan, then maybe it's not so important for others to become one. Maybe that role has already been filled.

But as it is, every one of us is responsible for becoming a neighbor to the world. If we do not become a neighbor, then all of our love for others is really just a convoluted love for ourselves, because everyone that we love will look, act and believe just like we do. When the Samaritan reached out to a half-dead man in the ditch, he was reaching out across cultural and religious lines to someone who was very different from himself.

All of this relates to what Jesus himself said earlier in his Sermon on the Mount:

> You have heard that it was said, "Love your neighbor and hate your enemy." But I tell you, love your enemies and pray for those who persecute you, that you may be children of your Father in heaven. He causes his sun to rise on the evil and the good, and sends rain on the righteous and the unrighteous. If you love those who love you, what reward will you get? Are not even the tax collectors doing that? And if you greet only your own people, what are you doing more than others? Do not even pagans do that? (Matthew 5:43-47)

A Neighbor to the Needy

Let's now consider the implications of this parable and the questions it raises. If I, myself, am the neighbor, then is this parable only about the individual people that I might happen to come across? Certainly it *is* that, but is it more than that? Yes! Wherever you go, if you *are* a neighbor, then you *create* neighbors.

Little reported in the media is the fact that Christians are often the first to arrive and the last to leave whenever there's a natural disaster. Whether heartache comes by means of a hurricane, tornado, earthquake, or some other disaster, Christians are often among the first-responders, making neighbors by becoming neighbors. That's because being a neighbor means being connected to other people. Jesus said, "I tell you the truth, whatever you did for one of the least of these brothers or sisters of mine, you did for me." (Matthew 25:40)

Karl Marx famously said, *"Die religion ist das opium des volkes,"* that is, "Religion is the opiate of the masses." He wrongly believed that the more religious that people become, the more they tend to focus on the "sweet by and by" and not the problems of the real world. In essence, their religion serves as a sedative, making then unconcerned about earthly things such as injustice and poverty. But Marx didn't understand Biblical Christianity. As Timothy Keller has written, "Christianity is by no means the opiate of the people. It's more like smelling salts."[4]

A Neighbor to Different Ethnic Groups

Another question raised by this parable is in the area of race relations. To what extent, if any, should I treat those of different ethnicities any differently from my own? Much has already been said about the racial tensions that existed between the Samaritans and the full-blooded Jews. It is no accident that the hero of this story turns out to be someone completely other than we would expect him to be. We would expect the hero to be the priest or the Levite. But the hero not only turns out to be a layperson, he's a Samaritan at that! What a shock this must have been.

There's really only one race—the human race. Caucasians, Blacks, Arabs, Jews, and Polynesians are not different races. They are ethnicities of one race, which is the human race. Every one of us is created in the image of God and as such, every one of us is entitled to dignity and respect.

The early church was a racially integrated church. Paul says in Galatians 3:28 that "There is neither Jew nor Gentile, neither slave nor free, nor is there male and female, for you are all one in Christ Jesus." That being the case, no one race can have preferred status over the other.

How tragic that there are still some people in America who believe the white race is somehow superior to all others! Those who would twist Christianity into a religion of white supremacy overlook how one of the earliest converts to Christianity in the Bible was a man from Ethiopia, who presumably had very dark skin color. (Acts 8:26-40) They also have difficulty with the man who carried the cross for Jesus. Simon was from Cyrene, a community of dark skinned people on the North Coast of Africa. (Matthew 27:32; Mark 15:21; Luke 23:26) Cyrene, incidentally, was also represented on the Day of Pentecost (Acts 2:10) and benefitted from early missionary work. (Acts 11:19) Later, in Acts 13, we find a list of prophets and teachers ministering at the church in Antioch. We're not only introduced to Lucius, another man from Cyrene, but also Simeon, whom they called "Niger," meaning "black." (Acts 13:1)

Despite the strong Jewish origin of the Christian Church, it very quickly became an inter-racial church. And that's just how God intended it to be, for the Great Commission sent Christians out into the whole world (literally, *panta ta ethnē,* to "all the ethnics") with the Good News of Christ. (Matthew 28:19) When we come to the Book of Revelation, we find that by the blood of Christ people came to God "from every tribe and language and people and nation." (Revelation 7:9) So there's no basis for discrimination, is there?

Indeed, in Ephesians 2 we read about two different ethnic groups (Jews and Gentiles) and how God brought them both together.

> For he himself is our peace, who has made the two groups one and has destroyed the barrier, the dividing wall of hostility, by setting aside in his flesh the law with its commands and regulations. His purpose was to create in himself one new humanity out of the two, thus making peace, and in one body to reconcile both of them to God through the cross, by which he put to death their hostility. He came and preached peace to you who were far away and peace to those who were near. For through him we both have access to the Father by one Spirit. (Ephesians 2:14-18)

The ultimate solution to racism cannot be found in laws designed to change people's behavior. In the parable that Jesus told, the priest and the Levite were both well educated in the law and yet it did not make them compassionate towards someone in dire need. Instead, the answer to racism is a changed heart. Such a change is only possible through Jesus Christ.

A Neighbor Beyond My Faith Community

Another troubling question raised by this parable is "How often does religion get in the way of God's compassion for all people?"[5] The priest and the Levite were both imaginary figures, created in Jesus' mind for the purpose of the story. Therefore, we shouldn't speculate too intensely on the reasons these hypothetical people might have had for passing by on the other side of the road. If there was a reason in the back of Jesus' mind, there's no way of knowing for sure what it might have been. Still, every pastor ought to be troubled that these two ministers failed the "neighbor test." They had no pity like the Samaritan did. Plus, as we'll see when we get to Luke 10:37, they demonstrated no mercy either. And yet, they were supposed to be God's representatives! In the end, God's work was not done that day by the priest or by the Levite, but by a Samaritan outcast.

We'd all probably like to think that God is working in our lives, accomplishing his will through us. If, however, we become unusable to God through hardness of heart, laziness or whatever, then God is more than capable of finding someone else through whom he can work. In addition, the exercise of God's compassion cannot be limited to us as individual people. It applies to the corporate culture of churches, too. If a church lacks compassion towards its own members and to those outside of its walls, it will soon find itself in decline. It will cease to be a safe and healthy environment for spiritual growth and service.

But it goes deeper than that. Life can get complicated at times. The law says not to do any work on the Sabbath (Exodus 20:8-11) and yet what if an emergency arises? On one occasion Jesus asked what they would do if someone's sheep should fall into a pit on the Sabbath. (Matthew 12:11) Compassion demands that you remove the sheep from the pit. If you can be compassionate towards a sheep, why can't you be compassionate towards another human being? Nevertheless, many of the Pharisees said, "No, you can't do it because it's the Sabbath and certain religious rules are in effect." Religion got in the way of God's compassion.

Jesus was accused on several occasions of healing on the Sabbath, something they viewed as work. When confronted about it, he merely observed, "It is lawful to do good on the Sabbath." (Matthew 12:12) A Sabbath rule was never intended to stand between someone in genuine need and another person who's ready, able and willing to help.

Earlier, Jesus and his disciples had been plucking grain as they walked along the wayside. Now, this was perfectly legal according to the law. Besides, there was a legitimate human need. They were hungry. But once again it took place on the Sabbath. The Pharisees were upset because, in their minds, Jesus and his disciples were breaking the Sabbath. They were harvesting grain! (Matthew 12:1-3)

Of course, when David and his companions went into the temple and were hungry, they had no druthers about eating the showbread that had been set out. Normally only the priests would eat the leftover showbread, but David and his companions were hungry so they ate. (Matthew 12:3-8) The religious rules have value, but there will be times when human need will outweigh them, because "The Sabbath was made for man, not man for the Sabbath." (Mark 2:27)

James Smart notes, "Every form of religion has in it the danger of becoming not a highway to God, but rather an obstacle between man and God, blocking the highway on which God seeks to come to man."[6] In this case, Sabbath rules became more important than people themselves. In an ironic twist, of the seven days in the course of a week, the Sabbath was the busiest for the priests and the Levites. *Somebody* had to work on the Sabbath and not just religious professionals, either. The same is true today. What about emergency medical personnel, or the police? If you saw your neighbor's house on fire, would you say, "Sorry, but I have a Bible study I want to attend?" No, you'd drop everything and call the Fire Department, perhaps wielding a hose until they arrived. The Parable of the Good Samaritan teaches us to never let so-called "religious duties" keep us from showing compassion.

A Neighbor to the World

And finally, as we broaden the application, can we appropriately apply this parable to the realm of international relations? Can this concept of neighborliness be extended to all the nations of the world?

The history of the world is the history of migration. Since the beginning of recorded history—even back to the Garden of Eden—groups of people have moved from one place to the next for a variety of reasons. The United Nations estimates that worldwide currently over 210,000,000 people migrate each year from one place to another.[7] This figure includes refugees, those seeking asylum and those who are simply seeking a better way of life. It also includes those who have migrated both legally and illegally. The issue of immigration is not merely an American issue. It is an international one.

Still, the flood of illegal immigration into the United States continues to be a major political issue in America. It is estimated that between 7,000,000 and 20,000,000 people are presently living in the United States without legal documentation, most of them having come across the Mexican-US border. Another 500,000 enter the country each year, but nobody really knows for sure.[8] The fact that the vast majority of these undocumented immigrants are of Hispanic ethnicity adds a racial dimension to this issue.

What is a neighborly response? Does being a good neighbor to these immigrants require acceptance of their illegal entry? What about the economic impact (both positive and negative) that such acceptance might have? Alan F. H. Wisdom answers,

> The oft-quoted command in Leviticus 19:33—"When a foreigner resides among you in your land, do not mistreat them"—should shape our attitude towards citizens of other countries. But the passage does not say how many aliens should be admitted into the United States today. It does not indicate whether one million "green cards" is too few, too many, or just the right number. Compassion for the foreigner does not necessarily mean opening our borders to all comers.[9]

While compassion is required from all Christians, the Bible does not provide a blueprint for immigration policy. Furthermore, we should be wary of too closely associating ancient Israel with the United States. Israel was a theocracy; America is not. In addition, the sojourners in ancient Israel were not illegal immigrants. Wisdom explains:

> [They were] permitted to pass through or reside in Israel. They were required to comply with Israel's laws and customs. In most cases they could not become Israelites. They could expect to receive basic justice, but not the full privileges of an Israelite.[10]

Martin Luther, who was greatly influenced by Augustine, argued that there are two kingdoms at work in this world.[11] One is a temporal (or political kingdom) and the other a spiritual kingdom. While both kingdoms are ordained by God, Luther saw the two functioning separately from each other. The civil kingdom deals with man's physical life in society as he interacts with other human beings. In this regard we are all subject to human governments. Nevertheless, the secular state's authority extends no further than to things related to a person's temporal life and property. On the other hand, Luther said there is also a spiritual kingdom that deals with a person's soul, which is eternal and subject only to God. This spiritual kingdom includes the church. We cannot expect the political government to adhere to Christian principles, for earthly kingdoms are "of the world."[12]

So we might well ask, "Does the teaching of the Good Samaritan apply to political relationships between countries?" I believe Luther would answer, "It could serve as a model, but secular governments don't necessarily operate under such spiritual principles." Still, it would be a mistake to think that Luther believed the church shouldn't influence government, especially where issues of the gospel are concerned. The relationship, then, between the church and the state is often ambiguous and ill-defined. This is especially true in America.

Still, as Christians we are called upon to "be subject to the governing authorities" (Romans 13:1) and to pray for our heads of state and governmental leaders. (1 Timothy 2:2) Christians are also called to be "salt and light" (Matthew 5:13) and neighborly in all of our dealings, for such relationships are a summation of the law. (Galatians 5:14)

D. H. Shearer

Neighborliness and Religion

It is clear that the Parable of the Good Samaritan is set within the context of faith. The lawyer is an expert in the Law of Moses. He asks about inheriting eternal life. He quotes Scripture and rightly interprets it. So the story is clearly told within a religious context. Nevertheless, there is nothing within the story itself that requires adherence to any specific religious creed. We have a priest and a Levite, but while their religious views may be assumed they don't seem to be a significant factor. What's more, we don't know what the religious views of the Samaritan were, or even of the man who fell among robbers. This parable is not primarily about orthodox belief. In the end Jesus' last words will be "Go and do likewise," not "Go and believe likewise," because we don't know what any of these characters believed. We can therefore conclude that being a good neighbor is something that transcends any one religion's teaching. Indeed, virtually every world religion teaches some form of the Golden Rule, which this parable describes.

Furthermore, we're reminded that even non-religious people may well be very moral. The Apostle Paul speaks of such people "who do not have the law, [and yet] do by nature things required by the law," becoming "a law to themselves." (Romans 2:14) In other words, everyone has some kind of a moral compass deep within them. Every society (whether Christian or not) has commonly held moral standards within itself. Hence, while the story of the Good Samaritan was originally told within a religious context, when taken strictly by itself one need not be religious to benefit from its moral teaching.

Still, as we've examined this parable of Jesus we have done so from a decidedly *Christian* perspective. As we have noted, many have sought to insert Jesus into the story by saying he typifies the

Good Samaritan.[13] Others have even associated Jesus with the victim. Nevertheless, as followers of Christ we cannot separate this teaching of Jesus from all of the other things he taught by his words and actions. Moreover, as Christians who seek to be ever "conformed into the image of [God's] Son," (Romans 8:29) we understand that Jesus calls upon us to emulate the Samaritan's example, for it is entirely consistent with the example we have received in Christ. So while the Good Samaritan may not directly represent Jesus, he certainly displays a Christ-like attitude and response to human need.

A Neighbor's Response: Mercy

This leaves us with just one last verse to examine in this parable. Jesus asked the lawyer which of the three people who came across the half dead man demonstrated the characteristics of a neighbor. The lawyer answered, "The one who had mercy on him." (Luke 10:37) Notice that he did not say "the Samaritan," but the one who demonstrated mercy. The lawyer understood the point behind the story, but he was still so racially and spiritually bigoted that he couldn't bring himself to even utter the word *Samaritan.*

Earlier in the story the Samaritan was filled with pity and we saw that the Greek word was *splanchnon,* or "bowels." But a different word is used now. Here the word is *eleos,* which is "mercy." There really is no good equivalent for *eleos* in English, yet it is an essential part of being a good neighbor. To show mercy is to support another person through a strong sympathy with him. As William Barclay wrote, it is "the ability to get right inside the other person's skin until we can see things through his eyes, think things with his mind, and feel things with his feelings."[14] We could add, "And to make his best interest my priority."

Can you think of a better kind of neighbor to have? Or to be? And Jesus said, "Go and do likewise." Amen.

Discussion

1. Tell about the people in the neighborhood where you now live. How well do you know them? What interests do you share? What differences do you have?
2. Identify who some of your closest friends have been over the years. What was it that drew and kept you together as friends? (Examples might include: hobbies, work associations, religious beliefs, life experiences, etc.)
3. In the Parable of the Good Samaritan, the one who proved to be a neighbor reached out to someone who was very different from himself. In your experience, who has been easier to get along with: someone who is very different from you, or someone with whom you have a lot in common, but has a few "quirks?" Explain.
4. If you had a deep, personal problem, which would you rather do? A) Talk it over with a close personal friend; B) Talk to a total stranger about it; C) See a pastor or a professional counselor; D) Keep it to yourself.
5. Martin Luther King, Jr. once said that 11:00 on Sunday morning (a traditional time for worship) was the most segregated hour in America. Do you agree? How closely does your congregation reflect the ethnicity of your community? Why is that?
6. James Smart is quoted as saying, "Every form of religion has in it the danger of becoming not a highway to God, but rather an

obstacle between man and God . . ." Do you agree? Have you ever seen it happen?
7. What would be the effect if the precepts of the Good Samaritan story were applied to America's immigration policy? What of America's foreign policy? Our dealings with terrorists? Would it be practical? Would it be desirable?

Chapter 6

Approaching the Parable of the Prodigal Son

Like the Parable of the Good Samaritan, the Parable of the Prodigal Son is one of the best known of Jesus' stories. Sometimes called "the Pearl of the Parables," it reflects "The Gospel within the Gospels." It is a story about how God's grace brings about redemption and restoration. It is also shows how some people become upset when God chooses to bestow his grace upon those they don't feel are worthy of it. In the end, we wonder if one of the reasons the story is so loved is because its message is so misunderstood! There are *two* lost sons in the parable, not just one. Most interpreters place the emphasis on the younger son, hence the traditional title, "The Parable of the Prodigal Son." However, if this title is any indication, then neither the elder son nor the father has received just consideration.

There are two parts to this parable. The first is Luke 15:11-24, where the younger son demands his inheritance, leaves for a far country, squanders it, returns to his senses and comes back to his father's waiting arms. The scene changes in the second half, found in Luke 15:25-32. The elder son becomes angry over his father's generosity and refuses to attend the celebration that is being held. Note that the younger son never even appears in this second scene. Therefore, to call this story "The Parable of the Prodigal Son," is probably not the best of titles, for it ignores half the story.

Perhaps the reason for emphasizing the younger son is because of the allegorical way in which this parable has historically been interpreted. It is easy to push any story or too far, so it is important to consider the context in which the parable was first told.

Outsiders and Insiders

As the stage is set, Jesus is teaching to a broad audience. There are "large crowds traveling with Jesus" (Luke 14:25f), including tax collectors and assorted "sinners." (Luke 15:1) Tax collectors were typically Jews who had allied themselves with Rome, using their position to extort unfair amounts of taxes and tolls from their fellow Jews. Since their income was based on the amount of money they brought in and since their assessments were without appeal, the profession was rife with corruption. Their place in Jewish society was further complicated by a controversy over whether Jews should be paying taxes to Caesar at all. (Matthew 22:15-22) The Jews considered tax collectors to be so dishonest that their testimony was not accepted in a court of law. In short, they were controversial, hated and often associated with prostitutes and other sinners.

Also in the crowd to whom Jesus was teaching were "sinners." Luke uses the term here in a generic sense, not referring to specific sins but to sin in general. These people failed to keep the Mosaic ceremonial law and its moral precepts.[1] Tax collectors and sinners were sometimes lumped together. (Luke 5:30; 7:34) In short, tax collectors and sinners were the classic outcasts of Jewish society.

In contrast, Luke records that Pharisees and teachers of the law were also in attendance. (Luke 15:2) If tax collectors and sinners represent the outsiders of Jewish society, certainly the Pharisees and teachers of the law were the insiders. They were strict observers of the law and honored by society for their fidelity. Jesus himself acknowledged that "The teachers of the law and the Pharisees sit in Moses' seat." (Matthew 23:2) They held positions of authority within Judaism. Each synagogue had a chair in its worship space representing the teaching authority of those who taught from the Torah.[2] Teachers in the synagogues would stand for the reading of God's word and then sit down to expound upon it. The chair in which they sat while teaching was euphemistically called "Moses' seat."[3]

The Pharisees were a select group of separatists, numbering about 6,000 at the time of Jesus. It was the strictest of all Jewish sects. (Acts 26:5) The Pharisees accepted both the Law of Moses and the Prophets as authoritative. They also developed a rigid and complex system of teachings and traditions on how the law should properly be observed.

The teachers of the law are sometimes called scribes (*grammateis*, the basis for the English word "grammar"). In the days before printing presses, they were the official copyists of the law. Because they worked so closely with the "letters of the law," they were experts on its content and so became authoritative interpreters of it.

As Jesus taught this mixed crowd of religious insiders and outsiders, we would hope that the insiders would want to reach out to the outsiders. But such is not the case. "... The Pharisees and the teachers of the law muttered, 'This man welcomes sinners and eats with them.'" (Luke 15:2)

In response, Jesus tells three parables about outsiders becoming insiders. That is, when lost objects (which ultimately represent people) are found. It's worth noting, however, that each of these three parables is nevertheless known by its negative rather than positive features.[4] In the titles they've traditionally been given, the focus is on the *lost* sheep, the *lost* coin and the *lost* (or prodigal) son. In contrast, in each case Jesus places the emphasis on the *restored* state of these items and the joy that accompanies it. We must never forget that the gospel is good news, not bad news.

A Lost Sheep

The first story is the Parable of the Lost Sheep. (Luke 15:3-7)[5] Jesus asks, "If you had 100 sheep and lost one of them, wouldn't you leave the 99 to fend for themselves in the open country and go in search of the lost sheep?" Of course, it would be risky to do so, but because each and every sheep is valued so much, it would be worth the risk. Jesus summarizes the attitude of the searching shepherd: "And when he finds it, he joyfully puts it on his shoulders and goes home. Then he calls his friends and neighbors together and says, 'Rejoice with me; I have found my lost sheep.'"[6] (Luke 15:6)

Jesus then gives the point of the parable: "I tell you that in the same way there will be more rejoicing in heaven over one sinner who repents than over ninety-nine righteous persons who do not need to repent." (Luke 15:7) The outsiders and insiders in Jesus' audience are both addressed. The outsiders (tax collectors and sinners) who repent are the cause of great rejoicing in heaven. But who are these "ninety-nine righteous persons who do not need to repent?"

While some have argued that the Pharisees and the teachers of the law were, in fact, righteous and did not need to repent, a better approach is to recognize the irony in Jesus' statement. There will be more rejoicing in heaven over one sinner who repents than over ninety-nine people who think they are so righteous that there is no need for them to repent.[7] When understood in this light both the outsiders and insiders, despite their apparent spiritual condition, stand in need of repentance. The simple truth is that nobody's perfect.

A Lost Coin

The second of the three parables Jesus told is found in Luke 15:8-10. The Parable of the Lost Coin also focuses on a lost object and the joy that comes when it is found. In this case a woman has ten silver coins and loses one of them. The monetary value of these coins is hard to determine. As Luke records the story, they're called *drachmas*. Together they're worth no more than ten denarii, or about ten days' worth of common labor.

William Barclay speculates that perhaps the reason this single coin was so valuable to the woman was because it was a part of her bridal veil.[8] Such a veil would be held to her head by means of a chain of silver coins. Thus, her chain of coins could carry the same emotional attachment as a wedding ring. The sentimental value would far outweigh the monetary value. In the end, however, it doesn't matter. Whether the coin is prized for its sentimental or monetary value, the result is the same. The coin is very precious to her, so she searches everywhere throughout the house.

Her thoroughness is emphasized in that she lights a lamp and sweeps the floor looking for it. Given the construction of houses at the time, lighting a lamp would be necessary even during the day. The average house had only one or two small windows, if they had any windows at all. Furthermore, the windows were made small enough to keep a prowler out or to minimize the effects of wind and rain. Sometimes bars or lattice work covered the opening, so a lamp would have to be lit in order to make a thorough search. Even then, the amount of light dispersed by a typical oil lamp of the day would be marginal at best, demonstrating the woman's commitment to finding the coin.

When she finds her coin, however, her response is the same as that of the shepherd who had lost one of his sheep. She calls all of her girlfriends and women of the neighborhood[9] and says, "Rejoice with me; I have found my lost coin." (Luke 15:9) Jesus' application of this parable is substantially the same as that of the lost sheep. Jesus says, "In the same way, I tell you, there is rejoicing in the presence of the angels of God over one sinner who repents." (Luke 15:10)

The role of community is a major theme in both of these parables and especially in the one that follows. The sheep is restored to the community of the flock, while the coin is restored to the community of the purse or bridal veil. Things on the outside become things on the inside. In addition, in both stories the one who finds the lost object goes to their friends to tell them the good news. Nothing exists in isolation in these parables.

> Nothing exists in isolation in these parables.

At the completion of these first two stories we can well imagine that the Pharisees and the teachers of the law were becoming a bit uncomfortable, wondering what might come next. Anyone with common compassion would be happy if a wandering, poor and defenseless sheep was restored to the flock. The same thing holds true for a lost coin. Who wouldn't be happy for this woman who searched so diligently? No one would begrudge her for her joy.

Of course, sheep and coins don't have the same moral baggage as tax collectors and sinners. Restoring a sheep to a flock or a coin to a purse is one thing. Sitting in church next to a known sinner is something else, even if that sinner has come to repentance. After all, people have reputations. Heaven might rejoice when lost people are found, but self-righteous Pharisees and teachers of the law might find it much more difficult.

A Lost Son

That's why Jesus tells a third parable in Luke 15:11-32. The basic premise is the same. Instead of a sheep or a coin being lost, the lost item is now a father's own younger son. The theme of community is once again central to the story. The younger son rejects the community of his father, family and friends. When he returns home in repentance, however, the elder son begrudges the celebration that takes place. It seems that not everyone rejoices when the lost are found. The younger son may have been restored to the family, but the parable leaves us wondering if the *entire* family (which includes the older son) can ever be brought back together again.

The Parable of the Prodigal Son has several broad allegorical elements. Still, to treat less important details in the story in an allegorical fashion does a disservice. It ignores the parable's context and diverts our attention away from the main points. The younger son who demands to go his own way, only to eventually return to his father, typifies a sinner. The father to whom he returns is God. And the elder son represents the Jewish leaders, specifically the Pharisees and the teachers of the law.

In strict allegory, however, everything in the story always stands for something else. Tertullian, an early Christian apologist, offered this explanation of the parable:

> The older son is the Jew; the younger son is the Christian. The inheritance which was shared is the knowledge of God which is man's birthright. The citizen in the far country who hired the younger son is the devil. The robe placed on the returning son is the sonship lost by Adam at the time of the Fall. The ring is the sign and seal of baptism, the feast is the Lord's Supper and the fatted calf is Jesus.[10]

Of course, when dealing with allegory, anything can stand for anything with very few restrictions. As T. W. Manson has noted, this parable was never intended to be a complete compendium of theology.[11] We should not push any parable too far. Allegorical interpretations can be so arbitrary and subjective that they can easily become far-fetched. Something as simple as water can mean literal water, baptism, moral purity, or even eternal life in the New Jerusalem.[12]

The Parable of the Prodigal Son illustrates that allegorical interpretations also lack any form of objective correction. The interpreter becomes the *de facto* authority (i.e. "It means whatever I say it means"). Who is to say which interpretation is right or wrong, appropriate or inappropriate? When allegory runs wild, the Bible becomes putty in the hands of whoever happens to be interpreting it. Care must be exercised. Nevertheless, as noted, the Parable of the Prodigal Son does have some allegorical elements in it, but those elements are appropriate given the context leading up to it.

We still haven't decided what a good name for this parable might be. To call it "The Parable of the Prodigal Son" all but overlooks the significant second half of the story. Focusing on the second half, Fredrick Danker has titled it "The Parable of the Reluctant Brother." One of the more provocative sermon titles also focuses on the elder son. It's called "How to Become a Prodigal Without Leaving Home."

Others, seeking to broaden the emphasis have suggested calling it "The Parable of the Two Lost Sons" or "The Parable of the Broken Family." Still others have pointed out that the one constant character in the parable is the father. So suggested titles are "The Parable of the Loving Father," "The Parable of the Waiting Father," and "The Parable of the Restoring Father." Timothy Keller observes that the word *prodigal* does not mean "wayward," but rather "recklessly spendthrift." In light of the way in which the father lavishly treats both sons in the parable, he certainly plays the role of a prodigal. If the father typifies God in this story, then perhaps we should call it "The Parable of the Prodigal God."[13]

Whatever we choose to call this parable, its message remains poignant for us today.

Discussion

1. By what title do you think we should call this parable?
2. Have you ever been in the midst of a large group of people where you felt out of place? Specifically, why did you feel so uncomfortable?
3. In the Parable of the Lost Sheep no particular reason is given for why the one sheep becomes separated from the rest of the flock. In your experience, why do you think that those who choose to leave a church do so? Is there usually a reason behind their decision, or do they just "nibble themselves away" without anyone contacting them?

4. Have you ever strayed away from the Lord? How were you restored to God and to his flock?
5. Why do you suppose we have traditionally emphasized the negative aspects of the three parables in Luke 15 (The *Lost* Sheep, The *Lost* Coin, The *Lost* Son)? Why not the positive aspects (The *Restored* Sheep, The *Restored* Coin, The *Restored* Son)?
6. What is the most precious thing that you have lost? Were you ever able to get it back? If so, how did you feel?
7. What do you think of Timothy Keller's suggestion that this story be called "The Parable of the Prodigal God?"

Chapter 7
The Seduction of Sin
(Luke 15:11-16)

What he did was reprehensible. It's hard to even imagine the rude brashness of the younger son, for it demonstrated his alienation from his father and family. Jesus begins the Parable of the Prodigal Son by simply stating: "There was a man who had two sons. The younger one said to his father, 'Father, give me my share of the estate.' So he divided his property between them.'" (Luke 15:11-12)

The Demand

This parable, like the Parable of the Good Samaritan, is so well known that it has become somewhat domesticated to us. It is hard for us to imagine the shock those who first heard it must have felt.[1] This younger son believed he would be better off living by himself apart from his father, but he had no resources of his own. His solution was to rudely demand that his portion of the inheritance be given to him right now, without waiting for his father to pass away. What he demanded was tantamount to a death-wish for his father. He was saying "I can't wait for you to die!" What kind of a son would ask for such a thing?

The Greek expression translated as "share of the estate" (*epiballon meros tēs ousias*) is not the normal phrase we would expect for an inheritance. It doesn't refer to fixed assets alone, but also to personal assets such as household goods, personal valuables, collections, etc. In short, the younger son asks for a total liquidation of all familial assets so that he can get what he feels is coming to him and to make a permanent departure. He wants to be "cashed out."[2]

Beyond the monetary aspect of his demand, there's a more important social aspect. He wants nothing to do with either his father or family in the future. All benefits and connections with them are forfeited. Like Esau before him, he sells his birthright for a pot of porridge. His action reflects an alienation that dishonors his father and causes great social embarrassment. In the social milieu of that time, his action also signals a break with the community at large. To renounce your father and family is to renounce all of their friends and associates. The breech between the younger son and his family and community is both real and severe. As the parable progresses, on two occasions the father will refer to his younger son as being "dead." (Luke 15:24, 32) He won't be exaggerating.

We might ask, "Where is the older son in all of this? Why doesn't he step in and intervene?" Within the culture of that day, we would expect the older son to assume the role of a peacemaker. Broken relationships were generally resolved through the intervention of a third party acting as an arbitrator, mutually selected by both parties. By reason of custom and the expectation of the community as a whole, the older son would have been pressured to assume a peacemaking role.[3] And yet he remains strangely silent. He is willing, however, to accept the eventual division of the estate which will also give him his share. His silence early in the parable is our first hint that his relationship with his father is probably no better than his younger brother's.

Dividing the Estate

In response to his younger son's demand the father "divided his property between them." The word used for property is the Greek word *bios,* which is better translated as "life." There are other, more distinct words that could have been used had the emphasis only been on material things. Instead, the father's life was torn apart when he "divided his life."

In ancient Israel a man's identity was closely connected to the property that he owned. As Timothy Keller observes, "To lose a part of your land was to lose a part of yourself and a major share of your standing in the community."[4] In essence, the land didn't belong to the family; the family belonged to the land. In the normal course of things, the land would remain in the family for generations, giving the family stability. A family's land or other major possession were protected by law and could be sold only in the most extreme and dire circumstances. But even then, during the year of Jubilee all familial lands would be returned. (Leviticus 25:23-34) In this way the family's ultimate tie with its property was protected.

Upon the death of the family's patriarch, the normal procedure for distribution would be for the father's older son to receive two thirds of the inheritance, with the remaining third being allocated to his younger son. (Deuteronomy 21:17)[5] Of course, this procedure assumes that the father has died, for "a will is in force only when somebody has died; it never takes effect while the one who made it is living." (Hebrews 9:17)

Still, while he was alive the father was free to do whatever he wished to do with his wealth. He decided to grant his younger son's demand, but then took it a step further. The father "divided his property between *them*." This means that the *elder* son also received his portion of the inheritance at the same time that the *younger* son did. But if that's the case, how can we account for the father's continuing management over the two-thirds of the estate that went to his elder son?

The formula for a pre-death distribution of assets was somewhat technical and not commonly employed.[6] A man could divide his estate by allocating capital while still retaining the income off of it. The recipient had full control over the capital. As long as he did not sell the capital that he had received, the giver would continue to receive the interest off of its investment. However, if the recipient should sell or otherwise forfeit the capital, the giver would no longer receive any income from the gift. What's more, the buyer of the capital could exercise no control over it until the death of the giver. Upon the death of the giver, however, whoever owned the capital would receive all future interest from it.[7]

So how did this complicated custom play out in Jesus' parable? In essence, the younger son was free to squander his share of the inheritance, but the inheritance itself only had the value of an "IOU" until his father died. In such a case, the inheritance would most likely have been squandered for pennies on the dollar and would be quickly exhausted. What's more, when it was gone, his father lost all future income off of it. When the younger son squandered his inheritance, it signaled the final cutting of all ties with his father.

In contrast, the elder son retained his inheritance. For all practical purposes, the fact that he also had received his share of the inheritance at the same time his younger brother did made no difference to him. Nothing had changed. He still lived at home and his father still controlled the interest off of it. The father continued to manage the estate.[8] This explains why the father will later have resources with which to celebrate his younger son's homecoming and will be able to say to his elder son, "You are always with me, and everything I have is yours." (Luke 15:31)

Gone for Good?

What went wrong with this younger son? Later in the parable his older brother will accuse him of squandering his share of the inheritance on prostitutes, but there's a sin here that's even more basic than that. We read, "Not long after that, the younger son got together all he had, set off for a distant country and there squandered his wealth in wild living." (Luke 15:13)

The words and phrases that Jesus used are powerfully descriptive. The younger son wasted no time in leaving home. His outward departure reflected an inner separation that had already taken place. His heart was far from home, so he "got together all he had," meaning that he took everything with him. He left nothing behind that would ever call him back and he had no plans of ever returning. The permanence of the separation is also suggested by the fact he left for a *distant* country. While a return home was possible, it certainly was not anticipated by this younger son. In his mind the break was complete. He had forfeited his name and his standing in the family and community, who now regarded him as dead.

Upon arrival in the distant country he began living life on his own terms. He "squandered his wealth in wild living." To squander (*diaskorpizō*) literally means "to scatter abroad." Elsewhere Jesus used the word literally,[9] but here it is a metaphor. Rather than focus on anything of practical value, he scattered his money, throwing it in all directions. He impulsively spent money on whatever struck his fancy at the moment. In the end, he had nothing to show for it.

He spent his money on "wild living," which signals why he wanted to leave home. There was a reckless quality to his spending. Beyond that, we are not given any details about what his new lifestyle entailed, except that his older brother would later accuse him of being with prostitutes. (Luke 15:30) We can imagine a hedonistic bent to every aspect of his behavior. In any case, his new lifestyle was far different from what he ever experienced at home with his father.

Tough Times

The story continues:

> After he had spent everything, there was a severe famine in that whole country, and he began to be in need. So he went and hired himself out to a citizen of that country, who sent him to his fields to feed pigs. He longed to fill his stomach with the pods that the pigs were eating, but no one gave him anything. (Luke 15:14-16)

His resources couldn't have lasted long. He might have tried to liquidate his assets before leaving for the distant country, or perhaps not. But in any case, remember that while his share of the inheritance could be sold, it couldn't be redeemed by the buyer until after his father's death. Therefore, it is highly unlikely that the younger son received full value for anything that he inherited. His inheritance was squandered in the very fact that he sold it for pennies on the dollar. To make matters worse, he was reckless in his spending, giving no thought to anything but his immediate enjoyment. Apparently the price was no object.

It was only a matter of time before he ran out of money. It was at this point that a second calamity came upon him. A severe famine struck the whole country. The younger son cannot be blamed for the famine,[10] but he certainly could have mitigated its effects by being more responsible with his money or by never leaving home in the first place. In any case, "he began to be in need." The basic necessities of life were no longer within reach. He was hungry, homeless and desperate. What's worse, he had burned all his bridges behind him. He had no friends and no support systems. No one cared what happened to him. He was all alone. But worst of all, his Jewish faith was waning within him, as will soon be seen.

Exploring the Options

At this point the younger son had four options open to him. The first was to beg for food. He was so hungry he would have gladly eaten the carob pods that the pigs fed upon. He apparently tried begging for pig slop "but no one gave him anything." The verb is in the imperfect tense, so a better understanding is "No one was giving him anything." In other words, he tried and tried and tried again, but it just wasn't working. He was a failure when it came to begging.

The second option was to find employment someplace. Of course, in tough economic times the competition for jobs becomes more acute. He had lived all his life as a child of privilege in his father's house. We wonder what, if any, marketable skills he had. How employable was he? Was he accustomed to physical labor?

He was a foreigner in a strange land. Would he be discriminated against?

If the job situation didn't work out where he currently was, then a third option would be moving on to someplace else. He could consider becoming a drifter, taking whatever odd jobs that might come his way.

The last option, of course, was to return home to his father. But how could he bring himself to do that? It certainly would be awkward. Besides, the younger son had too much pride to go home. He had cut all ties with home. He was on his own and totally independent. That's the way he wanted it. He had not yet reached rock bottom.

He chose the second option, getting a job with a citizen of that country feeding pigs. Now we begin to realize just how far away this "distant country" was. His employer was probably a Gentile, given the fact that he's called a citizen and not a mere resident of the distant country. Anyone could be a resident, but this employer was apparently a Roman citizen. It is true that some Jews such as the Apostle Paul and Silas were also Roman citizens,[11] but they were a statistical rarity. In addition, the fact that this citizen owned pigs assumes that he had a Gentile ancestry. We naturally make a different assumption about the younger son, however. We assume that he was Jewish just like everyone else who was listening to Jesus' parable for the first time. Being Jewish, perhaps he remembered the Scripture that says, "The pig... is unclean for you." (Leviticus 11:7) For a Jew to tend pigs is about as low as it can get.

He was surely caught in a quandary. He had to decide just how important this tenant of his religion was to him.[12] Jewish aversion to all things "unclean" was exceptionally strong. Could he rationalize tending pigs? If he refused to eat pork, could he still feed porkers? But what of the old rabbinic teaching which says

"Cursed be the man who would breed swine?"[13] Well, he wouldn't be breeding swine, only feeding swine. And so a rationalization, born of desperation, surely took place. It was a crisis of faith.

In the end, human necessity won out. He took the job. Perhaps he hated himself for doing it, but his pride wouldn't allow him to do anything else. He traded abundance in his father's house for poverty in a distant country. He traded freedom as a son for servitude as a hired hand. He traded family honor for the shame of degradation.

R. C. H. Lenski suggests that maybe the younger son's new boss didn't really want him as an employee. The New International Version says that "he hired himself out to a citizen of that country." (Luke 15:15) The word for "hired out" (*ekollēthē*) literally means that this younger son "glued himself" to his new boss. Perhaps he became such a nuisance that the boss finally relented and gave him a job with the pigs just to be rid of him.[14] If so, the pigs proved to be the only friends that this young man really had.

Symptoms vs. the Root Cause

So what was this younger son's sin? Several sins have already been suggested, among them poor financial management, visiting prostitutes, employment in an "unclean profession" and pride.

It seems that all these are really but symptoms of a much greater problem. At one time he was at home, living in harmony with his father. For whatever reason, he broke that relationship with his father and decided to set out on his own. William Richardson put it succinctly: "He was seeking to establish his life on his own terms apart from the father while using the father's resources."[15]

When the younger son demanded his inheritance he treated his father as if he was already dead. In all practicality, his father *was* dead to him. He wanted nothing to do with him. The relationship was severed, he thought, once and for all.

The rejection of his father was a repudiation of everything that his father stood for. What's more, it was a repudiation that began long before he ever left home. American novelist Winston Churchill concluded that the younger son's sin was "not the dissipation of appetite so much as the loss of his early inherited ideals and the gradual lowering of his standards of right and wrong."[16]

> "He was seeking to establish his life on his own terms apart from the father while using his father's resources." (William Richardson)

In short, the younger son's life was completely off target. The classic definition of sin (*hamartia*) is "to miss the mark." Sometimes sin refers to specific actions in the Bible, usually as measured by the Law of Moses. (Romans 7:7) In other instances sin is a principle at work which enslaves us. (Romans 3:9; 6:16-17; 7:7-12, 17, 21-22) In the case of the younger son, however, sin reflects an entire life that is off target. (Romans 1:18-23; Ephesians 2:1-3) The target was living in a harmonious relationship with his father and he fell short of it. In essence, he substituted his own goal for the one his father had intended for him.

He was "living in sin." In common usage today, the phrase "living in sin" is often applied to couples who live together without the benefit of marriage. Such a living arrangement, however, is a symptom of a much greater issue. While specific actions can be sinful, we often overlook the fact that when a life is off target and devoid of a harmonious relationship with God through Christ, the entire life is "lived in sin." Living in sin is living apart from the father.

In the first two parables of Luke 15, the break of relationship is evident. In the Parable of the Lost Sheep, the sheep is out of relationship with the shepherd and his flock. In the Parable of the Lost Coin, the coin is out of relationship with the woman and with all of the other coins in the purse. And now, in the Parable of the Prodigal Son, the son is out of relationship with his father, his family, and the community at large. That's the primary "life sin" of the younger son, which led him to all sorts of other specific sins (leaving home, squandering wealth, visiting prostitutes, etc.). If the younger son had enjoyed a harmonious relationship with his father he would have never left home in the first place.

We should remember, however, that the younger son did all of these things by using his father's resources. That is, he deliberately set out to live a lifestyle he knew his father would never approve of, yet fully expected his father to pay for it. The father has been severely criticized by some for giving in to his younger son's demands. Some have argued that father clearly knew that the son was leaving him, so he exercised codependency by enabling it to occur.[17] In essence, he financed his son's wayward activities.

Relationships and Risks

Certainly the father took a great risk in giving his younger son his share of the inheritance. He had no way of knowing that the inheritance would be squandered in such a way. But then, relationships always involve risk. Whenever we open ourselves up to love someone, there's always the danger that love will not be returned. To be created in God's image is to be a free moral agent, capable of making both good and bad decisions. A healthy, harmonious relationship can never be coerced or held together by force. There must always be the freedom to choose and to act independently within the framework of the relationship. This means that there's always the possibility that the relationship might be broken because of poor choices that might be made.

So was the father being codependent? He could have allowed his younger son to simply go his way, painful as the parting might be, without giving him a penny. Nevertheless, he acquiesced to giving him his share of the inheritance. Is this any different from a mother saying to her teenage daughter, "I don't want you to be sexually active, but just in case I want you to have these birth control pills?" Or a health organization saying, "Don't do drugs, but if you do we will supply clean needles at no cost to you?"

While the wisdom of such positions continues to be hotly debated, we must remember that we're not talking about pills or needles here. We're talking about an inheritance. From the father's perspective the inheritance was far more than mere money, although the younger son might have only seen it as such. The word "inheritance" (*klēronomia*) shares a common root with the word "heritage" (*klēroō*) in both Greek and English. Whatever was passed on from father to son had far more than material value. It represented the character of the one who passed it on.[18] You cannot disassociate the gift from the giver. As an example, Peter writes,

> Praise be to the God and Father of our Lord Jesus Christ! In his great mercy he has given us new birth into a living hope through the resurrection of Jesus Christ from the dead, and into an inheritance that can never perish, spoil or fade. This inheritance is kept in heaven for you ... (1 Peter 1:3-4)

The inheritance simply cannot be divorced from the One who made it possible, nor can it be divorced from his values. In this case, the inheritance comes as a result of the new birth and living hope that's ours through the resurrection of Christ.

As painful as it must have been to the father, when he acquiesced to his younger son's demand he was saying, "You may be repudiating me and all I stand for, but my love for you is so great that you will always be in my heart." Thus, the father could continually affirm his love for his son without ever compromising his own values or integrity. This is what elevates the father's action above birth control pills and needles. The division of property was a parting statement to his younger son about his heritage and identity. It also served as a reminder of the terrible immensity of the son's action. By all appearances, he had burned the bridge that led back home.

What Hath Sin Wrought?

When the younger son left home it was the culmination of an alienation that had begun much earlier. Of course, the parable doesn't tell us what the source of his dissatisfaction was and it is useless to speculate. The breech between him and his father was acute, however.

The sin of breaking his relationship with his father resulted in two terrible consequences. First, it brought slavery. The irony, however, is that in leaving home the son was not seeking slavery, but freedom. The Apostle Paul describes the situation like this:

> Don't you know that when you offer yourselves to someone as obedient slaves, you are slaves of the one you obey—whether you are slaves to sin, which leads to death, or to obedience, which leads to righteousness? (Romans 6:16)

Slavery in the ancient world was significantly different from our American experience with it. For one thing, slavery in America was racially based. No one ever thought of selling a white person into slavery. In the ancient world, however, people of all races became slaves as a result of war, kidnapping, or even by being sold into bondage by parents in order to pay off debts. In addition, in America there was always the assumption by slave-owners that their slaves were morally, intellectually and socially inferior. In the ancient world no such bias was prevalent.[19] Especially in urban centers, it was not uncommon for educated or skilled people to voluntarily sell themselves into slavery as a means of livelihood. They would negotiate a limited amount of freedom to earn what they could for themselves, but would always be under the "protection and care" of their master.[20] Of course, it also meant that they would no longer have any rights and ran the risk of being sorely mistreated. A slave was considered "living property."[21] The conditions under which a slave lived and worked depended solely upon his master. Manumission was possible, but not easily attained. In short, slavery was easy to get into, but hard to get out of.

The younger son foolishly yielded himself to a lifestyle that he thought would bring him independence, yet he discovered that it came with a terrible price. It was easy to get into, but very difficult to get out of. But then, that's how most destructive behaviors are, whether it is smoking, drinking, drug abuse, prostitution, gambling, exaggerating the truth, gossiping or whatever.

A second consequence of the younger son's action was alienation. He had cut all ties with his home with no right to ever return. He was both lost and as good as dead. His father will even recognize this fact at the close of the parable: "This brother of yours was dead and is alive again; he was lost and is found." (Luke 15:32) The younger son's insistence on going his own way estranged him from his father and everyone associated with him.

This section concludes with the younger son longing for the very carob pods on which the pigs were feeding and the sad words, "but no one gave him anything." He had hit bottom, living in a situation where no one in the world cared about him. Or so he thought.

Discussion

1. Was there a peacemaker in your family while you were growing up? If so, who? Now that you're an adult, has anything changed?
2. Do you think the father's willingness to give his younger son his share of the estate was a wise decision? What risks did he take?
3. Have you ever had a time in your life when "money was no object?" (This might include Christmas or vacations). How did it turn out?
4. The younger son moved away because he thought he would be better off on his own. How important is your personal independence and autonomy to you? Would a financial loan from a family member or friend change your relationship with them?
5. What does "living in sin" mean to you?

6. The younger son, sought to live life on his own terms apart from his father, while still expecting his father to pay for it. Have you ever given money to a friend or charity, only to later discover that it was not spent like you thought it would be? How did you feel? Did you do anything about it?
7. In dealing with the issue of codependency, the author leaves unanswered whether offering birth control to teenagers encourages promiscuity, or if offering needles increases illegal drug use. What do you think?
8. What legacy, whether material, intellectual, social or spiritual would you like to pass on to your children?
9. Where is God in this story?

Chapter 8

The Role of Repentance

(Luke 15:17-20a)

He had finally hit rock bottom, convinced that nobody cared. Reduced to eating the very carob pods that the pigs were feeding upon, he quickly discovered that no one was willing to give him the time of day. When he had money he seemed to have lots of friends, but now they had all abandoned him.

In the last chapter we briefly noted the options open to the younger son. He could try begging for food, but "no one gave him anything." Another option was to find employment, but working with pigs clearly wasn't working out for him. Or he could become a drifter, moving from place to place, seeking whatever odd jobs he could find. And, of course, there was always the fourth option of returning home.

Perhaps it was his pride that initially kept him from returning home. Or perhaps he simply realized that he had no right to return home. After all, he had burned his bridges. In essence, when he demanded his share of the inheritance he had wished his father was dead. When he squandered the inheritance, he further hurt his father by depriving him of any possible income off of it. With the inheritance gone, there was no longer anything that tied him to home. He had forfeited all standing with his father, his family and with the community at large.

Hitting Rock Bottom

Courtney Love, who herself has suffered from substance abuse and the effects of other poor choices, observed "I think you need to hit rock bottom before you make a decision about what you're going to do in the future."[1] That was certainly the case with the younger son. He was at the crossroads. His desperate situation gave him opportunity to reflect on what he had done and where his life was going. Why does it often take a calamity like this to wake us up to what's truly important in our lives? Fortunately, the younger son had an epiphany born of desperation.[2]

> When he came to his senses, he said, "How many of my father's hired servants have food to spare, and here I am starving to death! I will set out and go back to my father and say to him: Father, I have sinned against heaven and against you. I am no longer worthy to be called your son; make me like one of your hired servants." So he got up and went to his father. (Luke 15:17-20a)

The starting point for his journey home is found in Luke 15:17, where "he came to his senses." Literally it says, "he came to himself," which is an old Hebrew and Aramaic expression for repentance.[3] It's as if he looked at himself in a mirror and didn't recognize the image looking back at him. He saw someone who was living only for himself in a world of hunger, turmoil and destitution. He saw someone who had compromised everything in which he had ever believed. But worst of all, he saw isolation and loneliness. He had alienated himself from the father who loved him. In the process, he had also separated himself from the family and community he had always enjoyed.

As he looked at himself "he came to himself." He admitted that he had acted as if he was spiritually schizophrenic. He had to decide who he really was (or wanted to be), for if he didn't he would always be away from himself.[4]

The prodigal displayed a common human condition. Even the most dedicated Christian struggles from time to time with the challenge of consistently living the Christian life. The Apostle Paul admitted the warfare that existed within him when he wrote:

> So I find this law at work: Although I want to do good, evil is right there with me. For in my inner being I delight in God's law; but I see another law at work in me, waging war against the law of my mind and making me a prisoner of the law of sin at work within me. What a wretched man I am! Who will rescue me from this body that is subject to death? Thanks be to God, who delivers me through Jesus Christ our Lord! (Romans 7:22-25)

Like Paul and every one of us, the younger son had a choice to make about the kind of life he wanted to live and the relationships he would enjoy. But it wouldn't be easy because it forced him to face up to himself with brutal honesty. John Killinger observes:

> We have acquired the notion somewhere that we cannot afford to be honest, to be who we are, and that we must always take care to project some other image, the one we

think others—and God—would expect of us. We spend our lives hiding our real selves and putting forward our fabricated selves, our doctored alter-egos, our polite and respectable doubles.⁵

The younger son could no longer hide his "real self." His very identity was at stake. It was no longer just a question of his father's faith and morals, or of other people's expectations of him. His *own* faith, morals and expectations were on the line. He had been away from them while he squandered his inheritance. So, before he could ever come home to his father, he had to first come home to himself. He had to "come to his senses." He had to own up to what he had become and change his ways.

> Before he could ever come home to his father, he had to first come home to himself.

Repentance as Reorientation

The most common term in the Bible for "coming to your senses" is repentance. Surprisingly, the word repentance (*metanoia*) does not appear in this parable, but it is certainly described. Still, it *does* appear in the explanation of the preceding two parables in Luke 15 that set the stage for the Parable of the Prodigal Son. The Parable of the Lost Sheep (Luke 15:3-7) culminates with the words "I tell you that in the same way there will be more rejoicing in heaven over one sinner who repents than over ninety-nine righteous persons who do not need to repent." The Parable of the Lost Coin (Luke 15:8-10) concludes with "In the same way, I tell you, there is rejoicing in the presence of the angels of God over one sinner who repents."

Repentance has often been described in terms of turning around and going in a different direction. Perhaps a better understanding is that it is a reorientation of life. If sin is described as a life lived "off target" from God, then repentance is that which gets us pointed back in the right direction. It's like orienting a map. In order to enjoy the full directional benefit of a map, it must first be positioned in such a way that north on your compass corresponds to north on your map. With the map properly oriented, you can now strike out confidently, knowing you're headed in the right direction.[6]

To repent means that your life is now pointed towards God and everything else gets its direction from that orientation. This, of course, does not imply that future mistakes will never be made. However, the overall direction of your life will be one of seeking to please God. This reorientation requires three things.

A Change of Mind

In order to reorient your life there first has to be recognition that things are not properly aligned. The old adage rings true: "If it ain't broke, don't fix it." People don't generally make changes in their lives unless they feel a need to do so.

In the case of the prodigal son, he needed no convincing that his life was misdirected. He was hungry, living with pigs, living immorally, flat broke, and living apart from his father who still loved him deeply. So he "came to his senses." He changed his thinking about his lifestyle and his relationship with his father, neither of which was working very well.

Our justice system often sends convicted criminals to places called penitentiaries. The word, of course, is based on root *repentance*. Penitentiaries exist for two purposes: to punish past behavior and to reform future behavior. Sadly, the reformation doesn't always take place and the criminal reoffends. That's because it is possible for the penalty to be paid for past wrongs while still adhering to old thought patterns. Repentance requires a change of mind.

A Change of Heart

Repentance also requires a change of heart. The prodigal son could have tried to cut his losses by moving to another far country, perhaps even further away than the first one. He could have tried to start over someplace else and still remain alienated from his father. Clearly he had a change of heart. Simply put, he remembered what life was like back home when he enjoyed his father's love.[7] This was not merely nostalgia for the good old days. Nor was it primarily dissatisfaction with how his financial situation had turned out. He finally realized and appreciated how good life was back home.

Sometimes repentance is confused with sorrow. While a repentant person may well feel sorry for his actions, sorrow by itself effects no real change. As Paul wrote to the Corinthians, "Godly sorrow brings repentance that leads to salvation and leaves no regret, but worldly sorrow brings death." (2 Corinthians 7:10)

The distinction between repentance and sorrow is important because a person may feel terribly bad about the way his life is going and yet still not have a change of heart. The younger son hated his situation, yet he could have remained in the distant country with the pigs. He could have cursed the way in which he squandered his inheritance and abandoned his lifestyle of wine, women and song. He could have joined a "self-help" program, moved to another place, and tried to start over. He could have done all of these things and still not return to his father. Fortunately, he chose another course.

A Change of Behavior

The younger son came to realize that he could not repent of his rebellion against his father while still remaining in the distant country feeding pigs. He had to return home if any kind of reconciliation was to take place. Of course, at this point he had no idea how his return might be received. He had forfeited any and all rights as a son. Would his father hold a grudge? Still, he had to try.

If repentance is like reorienting a map, then the map must remain oriented if it is to be of any benefit. A change of mind and a change of heart requires a change of behavior. The Apostle Peter speaks of false teachers who, having held to the truth at one time, later deny it. He writes,

> If they have escaped the corruption of the world by knowing our Lord and Savior Jesus Christ and are again entangled in it and overcome, they are worse off at the end than they were at the beginning. It would have been better for them not to have known the way of righteousness, than to have known it and then to turn their backs on the sacred command that was passed on to them. Of them the proverbs are true: "A dog returns to its vomit," and, "A sow that is washed returns to her wallowing in the mud." (2 Peter 2:20-22)

The younger son's alienation from his father eventually led him to entanglement in the corruption of the world. If his repentance was true, he could not remain in the distant country. Otherwise, he would be no different from a dog returning to his vomit, or a pig going back to the mud after having been washed. He simply had to return home.

The Speech

We can imagine how nervous he must have felt. Have you ever dreaded a delicate or sensitive conversation with someone where choosing the right words were critically important? Maybe there was tension between the two of you, or you were called upon to give an account of your actions. Perhaps you rehearsed in advance exactly what you might say, so that when the critical moment came you wouldn't stumble over your tongue. That's exactly what the younger son did. He wrote, memorized, and rehearsed the speech he would give to his father upon his return. The words of the speech are given in the parable: "Father, I have sinned against heaven and against you. I am no longer worthy to be called your son; make me like one of your hired servants." (Luke 15:18b-19)

First he admitted that he had "sinned against heaven," which is another way of saying that he had sinned against God.[8] The Jews tended to use God's name sparingly, lest they risk breaking the commandment not to take God's name in vain, that is, in an empty or inappropriate way. (Exodus 20:7) Instead, they commonly used a substitute word such as "heaven."[9] Nevertheless, the meaning is clear: even though he never used God's name, the younger son had sinned against God. He had done so by his wild living, by breaking the Mosaic Law with pigs, and by visiting prostitutes.

He also admitted that he had sinned against people as well, specifically against his earthly father.[10] He did so by demanding his inheritance, by leaving home, by shunning his father's values, by squandering the inheritance and by depriving his father of any future income off of it. The fifth commandment of Moses is to "Honor your father and your mother." (Exodus 20:12) By bringing dishonor to his earthly father, the younger son also dishonored his heavenly father. He was right when he admitted "I have sinned against heaven and against you." He no longer felt worthy to be called his father's son.[11] He had no right to demand anything and he certainly was in no position to negotiate the terms of his return.

The final part of the younger son's speech was a request to be employed as one of his father's hired servants who, incidentally, were working under much better conditions than he was experiencing out in the distant country. The word for "hired servants" is *misthioi*, which denotes day laborers. (cp. Matthew 20:1-16) Such workers were hired on a day-to-day basis, with no promise of employment tomorrow. A day laborer had to prove his worth each and every day with no security for the future.

In terms of social status, to be a day laborer was even lower than a slave, for at least a slave was guaranteed food, clothing, and a roof over his head. Within first century Judaism, three distinct levels of status of servitude existed. At the top were bondsmen or "slaves of an upper class" (*douloi*). These could be household slaves who were considered a part of the estate and who might endear themselves almost as a member of the family. Beneath them were "slaves of a lower class" (*paides*), typically young, untrained or unskilled workers. These slaves would do menial labor such as working out in the fields. Lowest on the ladder were the hired servants (*misthioi*), who were complete outsiders as far as the estate was concerned and called upon only when needed. Although hired servants were free and not slaves, their position was precarious with no economic or social security whatsoever.[12] In fact, one of the laws of Moses protecting these workers required that payment be made to them at the end of each day of labor. (Leviticus 19:13) Thus, the risk of not being paid was limited to a single day's work. This lowest status of being a hired servant is all that the younger son could hope for.

After the shame and dishonor he had brought upon himself, upon his father and upon God, the younger son had no idea how his return home would be received. He failed to realize, however, how much his father still loved him despite his hurtful actions.[13] The father's love was unfailing, but he had separated himself from the full benefits of that love. Since the father's love was unconditional, his return did not make the father love him any more than he always had. Still, the son's return was absolutely necessary if he was to enjoy his father in any meaningful way.[14]

Going Home

This section concludes with the words, "So he got up and went to his father." (Luke 15:20a) Perhaps this was the hardest part. Writing and rehearsing a speech is one thing, but facing his father would be something else.

Discussion

1. Why does it often take a calamity to wake us up to what's really important in life, or to effect a change in things?
2. When it comes to the gospel, to what extent do you think people need to be told that they're sinners, or do they already know? Where does a person's consciousness of sin come from?
3. We often hear of "good people" who have done bad things. Do you think that people are basically good or evil? How do you account for good people who do bad things and vice versa? Is anyone really "good?"

4. If a person truly repents of a past sin, is it possible for him to go back and sin again by doing the same thing? Why is there such a discrepancy between what we want to do and our ability to do it?
5. Is it possible to repent of something and yet take no action?
6. The younger son came to the realization that he had sinned against both his father and God. Are transgressions against people always against God as well? Give some hypothetical examples.
7. Think back to the last speech that you gave. What was the occasion? Were you nervous? How did you prepare?
8. What is the lowest, dirtiest, nastiest job that you've ever had (paid or otherwise)? Why did you do it?

Chapter 9
In the Grip of Grace
(Luke 15:20b-24)

As we've seen, many titles have been suggested for this parable. The traditional emphasis has always been on the younger son, who demanded his share of the inheritance, went off into a distant country, squandered the inheritance on sinful living, and then returned to his father. Focusing on this younger son, the story has been commonly called "The Parable of the Prodigal Son," even though the younger son never appears in the second half of the parable. Others have rightly observed that there are really two prodigals in this story. The elder son was every bit as lost as his younger brother and yet he never left home. In more recent years, however, a number of scholars have emphasized the father as the key character in the story. After all, if there's one consistent person in the parable it is him. His steadfast love endured for both of his two sons.

Before continuing with the parable, it will be helpful to remember the context in which it is found. Luke chapter 15 begins with Jesus surrounded by tax collectors and "sinners." Apparently there were also a few Pharisees and teachers of the law standing off at a distance, muttering to themselves (loud enough for Jesus to hear) "This man welcomes sinners and eats with them." (Luke 15:1-2) Their criticism of the company that Jesus kept set the stage for three separate parables: the Parable of the Lost Sheep (Luke 15:3-7); the Parable of the Lost Coin (Luke 15:8-10); and the Parable of the Lost Son (or "Prodigal Son," Luke 15:11-31).

There several similarities in these parables. In each case something of great value is lost. That is, it out of place and not where it should be. A diligent search then takes place, followed by great joy when the lost object is found. But we should also note that in each case the lost object did not deserve to be found.

The sheep was lost when it nibbled itself away from the flock. It was probably unintentional. It could be argued that it was just doing what sheep often do, but it makes no difference. The result is the same. It was lost. In the same way, the coin was lost when it was separated from the rest of the coins of the purse. How it came to be lost is not explained in the parable, nor does it matter. The coin had no entitlement to be restored to the purse. But now, in the third parable the younger son becomes lost because of a willful choice on his part.[1]

If there is any merit in the Parable of the Lost Sheep, it lies with the shepherd who left his 99 other sheep in the open country and searched for the lost one until it was found. Likewise, if there is any merit in the Parable of the Lost Coin, it lies with the persistent woman who lit a lamp and swept the floor until she found it. Neither the sheep nor the coin deserved to be found. So in the end, it is grace that allows the lost to be brought back to where they ought to be.

The same thing holds true in the Parable of the Prodigal Son. The merit in the story rests solely with the father, who is anything but passive in his love for his younger son. Before the parable is over, both sons will find themselves in the grip of their father's grace.

However, in an interesting twist, we will be left hanging as to what the elder son wants to do about it.

The Son's Return

Jesus continues with the story: "But while he was still a long way off, his father saw him and was filled with compassion for him; he ran to his son, threw his arms around him and kissed him." (Luke 15:20b)

Some have suggested that this was a "divine coincidence." That is, the father just happened to be in the right place at the right time as his younger son came over the horizon. It is hard to be too dogmatic on this point since this story, like all of Jesus' parables, is a work of fiction created for teaching purposes. Still, we need to remember that Jesus was a master story-teller. He would probably not add useless and unnecessary information that would only serve to confuse his listeners. In short, there is a reason why the father sees his son while he is still far off. We can assume that the father has been out there, day after day, watching and waiting for his son to return. Despite his son's erring ways, the father has never given up on him.

This commitment on the part of the father is what this parable is really about. It is about the restoration of a relationship that was lost when mankind decided to go its own way. All of the vestiges of sonship were forfeited and only through the father's grace could they be restored.

As the story resumes, the father can't contain himself. Before his younger son has a chance to begin his prepared speech, he is filled with compassion. He is moved internally when he sees his son.[2] Forgetting all dignity, the father runs to him. We can well imagine the scene. This dignified, older man is a wealthy landowner and has many employees working for him. He's wearing long, flowing robes in the custom of the day. Normally, a gentleman would walk in public slowly in his robes. When going on a journey, he might "gird up his loins," which meant he would gather the lower parts of his garments up to his waist and tie them back, thus allowing freedom of movement and agility. But while practical, girding up loins always had a certain amount of humiliation attached to it.

Jesus doesn't mention whether the father girded up his loins or not, but either way the scene is noteworthy—an older man running full speed, either with robes flowing every which way, or else (if girded) with white, knobby, bare knees pumping up and down as he runs. No wonder Aristotle wrote that "Great men never run in public."[3] Is he panting? Is he out of breath? Is he sweating? Does he even care how he appears to others?

When the two finally meet, the father throws his arms around his son. Literally, the Greek text says that "he fell on his neck," an idiom showing heart-felt emotion.[4]

The father kisses his younger son.[5] Kissing among family members was common and denoted love and affection. The root of the Greek word for kissing is *phileō*, or "brotherly love." Under normal circumstances it is hardly surprising that a father would kiss his son, except that these are not normal circumstances. In light of the son's radically antisocial behavior, we might expect the father to keep an emotional distance.[6] But that's not what happens. The kiss is significant because at the time it takes place the father knows nothing about the little speech that his son has prepared. He knows nothing about his son's state of mind. He doesn't even know why his son has returned. For all he knows, his son has returned to ask for a greater share of the inheritance. Or perhaps he has returned with a list of grievances to be negotiated and resolved as a condition for him staying home. Yet to the father all of these concerns are overshadowed by the one single overriding issue: His long lost son has returned home!

Jesus continues:

> The son said to him, "Father, I have sinned against heaven and against you. I am no longer worthy to be called your son." But the father said to his servants, "Quick! Bring the best robe and put it on him. Put a ring on his finger and sandals on his feet. Bring the fattened calf and kill it. Let's have a feast and celebrate. For this son of mine was dead and is alive again; he was lost and is found." So they began to celebrate. (Luke 15:21-24)

The son begins his rehearsed speech, but the father doesn't want to hear it. He cuts him off. The son never has a chance to humbly request to be hired on as one of his father's day workers.[7] Instead, the father asks for four things to be given to his son: the best robe, a ring for his finger, sandals for his feet, and a huge BBQ in order to celebrate. These four items are tokens of honor and status, given to the younger son as a sign of his return to his father and family.

The Robe

There were various kinds of robes in the ancient world, just as there are today. The father calls for a *stolē*, which was a long robe worn generally on special or ceremonial occasions. It might be compared to an academic robe, or to the robe that a judge would wear in a courtroom. In countries associated with the British Commonwealth, it could be compared to the regalia worn by the mayor of a city.[8]

In this parable, the robe is described as "the best robe," or literally "the first robe." In other words, this robe is "first in quality," not "the first robe you can find."[9] The robe probably belongs to the father himself, but in any case it demonstrates the father's intention to welcome his son back as a full and honored member of the family. It may be that after so much time feeding pigs in the distant country, the younger son's clothing was soiled and barely presentable. If so, the father rectified that situation and made a clear statement at the same time: "This is my son and he is a full part of the family."

In the waning days of the American Civil War when victory seemed all but certain for the North, politicians hotly debated the terms and conditions by which the South should be restored to the Union. Many wanted to punish the South severely for the war, but when Abraham Lincoln was asked concerning his policy he was much more lenient. "I will treat them as if they had never been away," he said.[10] When the father called for a robe to be given to his younger son, he treated him as if he had never been away.

The Ring

The ring is another token of sonship. Specifically, it denotes authority. The ring placed on the younger son's finger was probably a signet ring which would contain the family crest, symbol, or name. Important documents were sealed with clay—today we would use wax—and an imprint would be made, guaranteeing the authenticity of the document and the approval of the owner of the imprint. Furthermore, it was not to be tampered with.[11] To give someone your signet ring was the equivalent of giving him power of attorney.[12]

When the father called for a ring to be placed on his younger son's finger, it signaled the restoration of all the familial authority that he had once possessed, including authority in household affairs and perhaps over day laborers out in the field. Even more important, it included authority granted by the father in financial matters as well.[13] When we consider how the younger son had squandered his wealth in the past, this aspect of his reconciliation becomes especially significant.[14]

The Sandals

Sandals were an expensive item in the ancient world. They were of simple construction, consisting of a flat leather sole, tied to the foot by means of straps. Slaves and poorer common laborers did not wear sandals, nor could they afford to do so. After a long period in the distant country, we can assume that the younger son arrived home bare footed.

In his rehearsed speech, the younger son had intended to ask for a job as a hired day laborer, someone whom we would presume to be without sandals. Of course, his father cut him off and didn't want to hear a word of it. The message the father gave was clear: "You will be treated as an honored son in my house and not as a common servant." Thus, the sandals were yet another token of the younger son's restored status in the family.

The old spiritual "Heav'n, Heav'n," speaks of the plight of African Americans held in slavery, but who nevertheless looked forward to better conditions in eternity. Among other things, the song says that "all of God's *chillun*" will eventually have shoes and a robe, which symbolize full acceptance into God's family. In contrast, the spiritual also suggests that not everyone who talks about going to heaven (presumably white slave holders) will eventually wind up there.[15]

The Celebration

The father exclaims, "Bring the fattened calf and kill it. Let's have a feast and celebrate!" (Luke 15:23) Meat was a luxury in the ancient world, generally consumed by the upper classes. Wealthy households could afford to keep a calf (whose meat would be especially tender) "fattened up" and ready for upcoming celebrations.[16] The mere fact that the father has such an animal on hand and available to him suggests that he had been anticipating his son's return.

Who was invited to the celebration? While some believe that only the family and the servants were involved, it is more likely the entire community was invited. They came when they heard the sound of the music. We must remember that the younger son's action had been a scandalous embarrassment to his father in the eyes of all of his friends and associates. What's more, when the younger son rejected his father he rejected those same friends and associates. A public celebration would not only publicize that the family has been restored, it would also serve to reconcile the younger son to the entire community whom he also alienated. Besides, a full calf can feed upwards to 100 people and in the days before refrigeration it would typically all be eaten at once.[17]

The feast is but a part of a greater celebration, however. The celebration also includes both music and dancing. (Luke 15:25)

It's ironic that the younger son, who had squandered everything he had on wine, women and song, now finds himself at the center of a wholesome celebration. While he was in the distant country he probably attended numerous parties as long as he could afford to do so. But they were far different from what he was now enjoying. His misguided quest for freedom had only brought him slavery. The impromptu party thrown by his father stands in stark contrast to anything he experienced while in the distant country.

The King James Version says that "they began to be merry." The word used is *euphranthōmen,* which literally means "to be mindful of a good thing." In other words, there was a reason behind the celebration and everyone except the older son understood what it was. (Luke 15:26-27) The father articulates the rationale for the celebration by saying "This son of mine was dead and is alive again; he was lost and is found." (Luke 15:24, 32)

Dead, But Now Alive

It would be easy to gloss over the father's feelings about his son's past behavior. After all, he cut him off in the midst of his rehearsed speech. He did not force his son to grovel or try to humiliate him. We might misinterpret events and think that nothing matters to the father except that his son has now come home. We might mistakenly think that the father views his son's actions as nothing more than "water under the bridge." There's a subtle danger of assuming that because the father's grace is so freely given, a person's conduct is of little consequence. Nevertheless, in this story the son's terrible behavior is presented as a stipulated fact and is never dismissed. So there's a tension here. On the one hand the younger son has clearly sinned, yet on the other hand the father greatly loves his son.

Forgiveness weighs these two factors out. Forgiveness says, "My love trumps your sin." That is, our relationship is more important to me than any grievance you might have committed against me. As LeRoy Lawson observes, "Forgiveness breaks the chain of eye for eye, tooth for tooth. You never get even in a cycle of retaliation; you just keep refueling the battle."[18] Forgiveness does not hit a reset button and turn back the hands of time. You can't rewrite history or change what has already taken place. If the relationship is to be restored it must be on terms that acknowledge both the sin and an overwhelming love.

As Desmond Tutu reflected on the younger son's behavior and the father's love, he concluded:

> At the risk of getting myself in trouble, I will say that in a sense it doesn't matter what we do. For nothing we can do, no matter how bad, will change God's love for us. But in another way it does matter, because when you are in love you want to please the one you love. Only those who have not been in love don't know how demanding love can be as we try to please the one we love . . . [19]

Therefore, to even consider "sinning that grace may increase" is to misunderstand what grace is all about. (Romans 6:1-2) To suggest, "I might as well sin because God will forgive me anyway" is to misunderstand both the nature of forgiveness and the relationship a Christian has with God. A terrible transgression has taken place that cannot be ignored. To willfully sin in anticipation of God's grace and forgiveness is to presume upon a relationship that might very well be in peril. (Hebrews 10:26-27) The celebration did not take place simply because the son had now returned from a long trip. Figuratively speaking, the son had actually died. He had cut himself off completely from his father and from his family. And what's more, the younger son realized what he had done. The father also fully realized the ramifications of his son's hurtful actions. There's no whitewashing or minimizing the impact of the younger son's actions. The father's willingness to extend his forgiving grace to his son is so powerful that it can only be described as "giving life to the dead."

The father's bestowal of grace typifies what God has done for every Christian:

> As for you, you were dead in your transgressions and sins, in which you used to live when you followed the ways of this world and of the ruler of the kingdom of the air, the spirit who is now at work in those who are disobedient. All of us also lived among them at one time, gratifying the cravings of our flesh and following its desires and thoughts. Like the rest, we were by nature deserving of wrath. But because of his great love for us, God, who is rich in mercy, made us alive with Christ even when we were dead in transgressions—it is by grace you have been saved. (Ephesians 2:1-5)

When the father offered grace to his younger son, he did not ignore the son's sinful actions. Indeed, the offering of grace recognized that a breech in their relationship had, in fact, taken place. To offer grace, therefore, is an act of judgment. Where there is

> When the father offered his grace to his younger son, he did not ignore the son's sinful actions. Indeed, the offering of grace recognized that a breech in their relationship had, in fact, taken place.

no transgression, there is no need for forgiveness. To claim God's grace without an acknowledgement of personal sin is pointless. Without an infraction, who needs forgiveness?[20]

Still, the Christian need not wallow in past sins. Paul asks, "We are those who have died to sin; how can we live in it any longer?" (Romans 6:2) Peter speaks of those who are "nearsighted and blind, forgetting that they have been cleansed from their past sins." (2 Peter 1:9) We must not live in the past. Nevertheless, we must also never lose our gratitude for what God, our Father, accomplished for us at Calvary. For as Jesus said, by faith in him we have "crossed over from death to life." (John 5:24)

How Free is Forgiveness?

Those who see the Parable of the Prodigal Son as an allegory of redemption are troubled by what the parable does *not* say. Forgiveness is freely given and the younger son repents when he "comes to his senses." However, missing is the presence of any atonement in the story.[21] The father merely accepts his younger son back on the basis of his willingness to return, without paying any additional price. If the main point behind the story is that the father (God) is willing to welcome his children (prodigals) home, what of Jesus' death on the cross which makes it all possible? As the Apostle Paul will later write, "Christ's love compels us, because we are convinced that one died for all, and therefore all died . . . God was reconciling the world to himself in Christ, not counting people's sins against them." (2 Corinthians 5:14, 19)[22]

One of the dangers in interpreting parables, however, is attempting to make the story say too much. As Robert Stein notes, "One cannot require in a parable such as this, which teaches God's love for the outcasts and the hostility this encounters, a complete doctrine of the atonement as well. A parable is not meant to serve as a shorter catechism of all Christian doctrine."[23] In addition, no passage of scripture should ever be interpreted at the exclusion of other relevant passages in the Bible. Just because the Bible does not mention something in one passage doesn't mean that it must be silent in all others. Furthermore, an argument based on silence (i.e. what the Bible means by what it doesn't say) is generally recognized as the weakest of all arguments.

God welcomes all kinds of sinners when they come home. The terms of his acceptance are not the thrust of this parable and are therefore, not included in Jesus' story.

Lost, But Now Found

As we've seen, to be "lost" in the three parables of Luke 15 simply means "to be out of place." In the Parable of the Prodigal Son, the younger son belonged at home with his father, not out in the distant country. In addition, being where he belonged required a relationship with both his father and with his father's family. It wasn't enough that the younger son could repent, come home, and be reconciled with his father. If it was, then the parable would have ended at Luke 15:24.[24] Instead, the second half of the parable focuses on the older son who, like his father, has also been deeply hurt by the prodigal's behavior. If both sons are to live harmoniously with their father, they must be reconciled with each other.

In the final analysis, as much as we like to sing *Amazing Grace*, this parable is not ultimately about God's grace. Rather, it sees grace as the means to an even greater end: *the restoration of a broken relationship with God and with his family.*

Discussion

1. The author states that if there is any merit in the lost objects of Luke 15 being found it rests with the one who does the looking and not with the objects themselves. Is that always the case? What role did human effort play in God finding you?
2. How do you explain the father in this parable seeing his younger son while he was still so far off in the distance? Was it mere coincidence or something more?
3. Tell about a time when you were so moved emotionally that your stomach was tied up in knots.
4. How demonstrative in showing affection were people in your family while you were growing up? Have things changed?
5. Are there any tokens or heirlooms that you own that signify you are a member of your family? (e.g. jewelry, china, traditions) How did you come by them?
6. Where was the last *public* BBQ that you attended? What was the occasion? Was there entertainment of some sort?
7. Do you think the father went too easy on his son?
8. Some Bible interpreters believe that the younger son never truly repented and that upon receiving the tokens of sonship from his father (robe, ring, sandals, BBQ), his attitude was "Ha! I outwitted you again!" Do you agree or disagree? Why?
9. Is it possible to forgive someone who has shown no remorse for what they've done? What if they have died?
10. Tell of a debt of which you've been forgiven. How did it make you feel?

Chapter 10
Grumbling About Grace
(Luke 15:25-30)

He was upset and voiced his anger freely. And why not? In his mind he had been treated shabbily by the one who should have given him the kindest consideration—his own father. After all, he had stayed at home, loyally serving his father day after day while his younger brother took off for parts unknown, engaging is all sorts of sordid behavior. And yet now an impromptu party is in full swing—a party complete with a BBQ, music and dancing—celebrating the fact that his wayward brother has come home. It just wasn't fair.

This chapter focuses on the older brother's reaction to the grace extended to his younger, undeserving brother.

His Discovery

> Meanwhile, the older son was in the field. When he came near the house, he heard music and dancing. So he called one of the servants and asked him what was going on.

"Your brother has come," he replied, "and your father has killed the fattened calf because he has him back safe and sound." (Luke 15:25-27)

As he often does, Jesus utilizes "The Rule of End Stress." There's a major twist near the end of the story that comes as a surprise and where the main thrust of the story is generally found. That a wayward son would be welcomed home by his father might seem generous and normal enough, but to throw a party on his behalf was really over the top!

This section begins with the older son out where he has always been—in the field, dutifully serving his father. Of course, we're not told what he had been doing out there, but we can assume that he was working in a managerial role and not as one of the hired hands. This assumption is logical, despite his later claim that he's been nothing more than a slave for his father. (Luke 15:29)

Apparently it is quitting time, which explains why "he came near the house." The day's work is completed and it is now time to go home. Perhaps he is hot, tired, hungry and not in the best of moods. As he approaches the house, however, he can smell the BBQ and hear music and dancing off in the distance.[1] The musicians and dancers are most likely professionals who were hired at the last minute for entertainment purposes.

Clearly, something of importance is going on. Why hadn't he, as the older son, been notified? Perhaps the reason was simple enough—that the estate was so large he simply couldn't be located. But still, as the older brother of the guest of honor he should have been apprised of the celebration. In fact, he probably should have organized it. Or had he been snubbed? Was his father afraid that he would be angry enough to make a scene, or perhaps to even prevent the celebration from taking place? Whatever the reason, we have another clue of an important family dynamic. The older son wasn't any closer to his father than his younger brother had been.

He asks one of the hired servants, "What's going on?" The verb tense shows continued action. He can hardly believe his ears, so in disbelief he asks again and again. Finally the answer begins to sink in and it cuts him like a dagger: "Your brother has come and your father has killed the fattened calf because he has him back safe and sound." The one who has caused so much heartache within the family is now the reason for a great celebration. How can it be?

Hearing the words "your brother" must also sting his ears, for nowhere in the parable does the older son acknowledge that he even has a younger brother. The closest he will come is to refer to him as his father's son. (Luke 15:30) As far as the older son is concerned, his younger brother is dead and buried. He has done what his father refused to do. He has written him completely out of his life.

To make matters worse, the younger son has returned "safe and sound." Literally, the Greek word means that he has returned in a healthy condition.[2] In short, he doesn't seem to be any worse for wear. In spite of his dissipation in the distant country, by all appearances he still looks like his old self. It's as if nothing has changed!

But there's another issue at play here. Because of familial love, perhaps he can understand how his father might accept his younger brother back into the family. However, throwing a party and treating him like a conquering hero is nothing short of scandalous. Fred Craddock describes the situation well:

> It was the music and dancing that offended the older son. Of course, let the younger son return home. Judaism and Christianity have clear provisions for the restoration of a penitent returnee, but where does it say that such

provisions include a banquet with music and dancing? Yes, let the prodigal return, but to bread and water, not fatted calf; in sackcloth, not a new robe; wearing ashes, not a new ring; in tears, not in merriment; kneeling, not dancing.[3]

Craddock continues by asking, "Has the party cancelled the seriousness of sin and repentance? We might even ponder whether, had we lived next door, we would have attended the party."[4] Presumably going to the party would imply a lackadaisical attitude about sin, or perhaps even as a blessing of his behavior.

His Disgust

> The older brother became angry and refused to go in. So his father went out and pleaded with him. But he answered his father, "Look! All these years I've been slaving for you and never disobeyed your orders. Yet you never gave me even a young goat so I could celebrate with my friends. But when this son of yours who has squandered your property with prostitutes comes home, you kill the fattened calf for him!" (Luke 15:28-30)

The older brother interprets the celebration as a personal insult. He's humiliated. The New International Version says that the older brother "became angry." Perhaps a better understanding is that he "was angry." The Greek word denotes a long-term anger that is nursed over time.[5] In other words, he had been angry about the whole situation long before his younger brother returned and long before he heard

> The older brother interprets the celebration as a personal insult.

music and dancing. We surmise that the seeds of his anger had been planted even before his younger brother demanded his share of the inheritance and left home. In any event, the older son refused to go inside and join the celebration. We can imagine the guests listening in while the older son argues with his father outside. His refusal to join the celebration serves as an additional humiliation to his father. But then, in this parable *both* sons humiliate the father at one time or another and both initiate a breech in their relationship. Therefore, both stand in need of their father's forgiveness.

As Luke crafts together the three parables of Luke 15, we're reminded of how he sets the stage for these stories at the very beginning. We remember that tax collectors and "sinners" had gathered around to hear Jesus, but the Pharisees and teachers of the law complained "This man welcomes sinners and eats with them." (Luke 15:1-2) Careful readers of Luke's Gospel can't help but to make the connection. The younger son would have been one of the sinners with whom Pharisees and the teachers of the law refused to eat. Jesus, in contrast, seemed to have no qualms about being seen with such people. The older son who refused to join the celebration identified with the Pharisees and teachers of the law, while the father acted more like Jesus. He welcomed sinners and ate with them.

It's also noteworthy that the father now takes the initiative to go and search for his older son. His goal has always been to bring his entire family together. Earlier in the parable the father looked for his younger son, day by day, off in the distance, hoping he would come home. But now, it's his older son that's missing. When he finds him he pleads with him to come inside. The verb is in the imperfect tense, showing continued action. He continues to plead, over and over again.

The Apostle Paul will use this same word and verb tense in 2 Corinthians 5:20, where he writes "We are therefore Christ's ambassadors, as though God were making his appeal through us. We implore [plead with] you on Christ's behalf: Be reconciled to God." God still pleads through the apostolic witness, begging people to be reconciled with the Father. Of course, he never overrides the individual's freedom of choice. The father will not force his older son to join the celebration if he refuses to do so.

The older son now begins to vent his anger, but before we examine what he says, we should note what goes unsaid. Up until now in the parable the father has been always addressed by his title as "father." (Luke 15:12, 18, 21) We observe that even when the younger son demanded his share of the estate he used this title of respect. But in the first words that the older son speaks there is no such politeness or courtesy. His first word is a belligerent *Look!* as if to say "Listen to me, old man!"

He feels humiliated by his father, especially in light of all of the years of faithful service he has given him. He says, in effect, that "he regarded his relationship with his father as one of slavish bondage instead of the free and spontaneous relationship of a child."[6] Perhaps this is hyperbole on the son's part, but feelings expressed in anger are often exaggerated. Looking ahead in the story, the father will assure him that he has always treated him like a son. (Luke 15:31)

What's more, the older son claims that he has always been an obedient son who has never disobeyed his father's orders. Again, this is most likely intended as hyperbole, for it is highly doubtful that he has *never* disobeyed his father one single time.[7] In any case, he sees himself as standing in stark contrast to his wayward and deadbeat younger brother. He believes the pattern of his behavior has been both exemplary and unappreciated. After many years of playing by the rules and keeping his nose clean, he has yet to receive even so much as a BBQ featuring a roasted goat![8]

Goat meat, even that of a young kid, is often tough and sinewy in texture. In some areas it is considered somewhat of a delicacy, such as among the Turkana people of Kenya. Most of the missionaries to that country that I've met tell me it is only considered a delicacy because of the absence of any better meats! Still, there would be no comparison between eating goat meat vs. eating the meat of a fatted calf.[9] Clearly the older son saw goat meat as being greatly inferior in quality. Even so, to add insult to his injury, he feels that his father has withheld even second-rate goat meat from him.[10]

In the original Greek text, the older son places himself in the emphatic position. Literally, he says "*to me* you never gave a young goat," showing how he feels he has been slighted. It's not about the calf or the goat, but what they represent. The self-centered attitude of the older son is apparent.

In addition, we should not overlook that older son also feels deprived of an opportunity to celebrate with his friends. Just as the meat of the fatted calf stands in stark contrast to inferior goat meat, so the upstanding friends of the older son are morally superior to the degenerate friends of his younger brother. But then, as Leon Morris observes, "The proud and self-righteous always feel they are not treated as well as they deserve."[11]

Finally, the older son charges his younger brother with squandering his father's property on prostitutes. We should first note that he refers to his brother as "this son of yours," as if to distance himself from him. Normally the natural flow of language would find him referring to his brother by his proper name. However, since no names are used in the story we would at least expect the older son to call him "my brother"—something he cannot bring himself to do. By referring to him as "this son of yours" the older son self-righteously separates himself, not only from the actions of his younger brother, but from his very person.

Earlier we saw that when the younger son demanded his share of the inheritance, in essence he was saying to his father, "I wish you were dead." (Luke 15:12) Now, the older son demonstrates this same attitude towards his younger brother. In his mind he no longer has a brother. He is dead to him.

As to the charge of squandering his father's property on prostitutes, it is best understood as being *devoured* by prostitutes. Or, as we might say, "his father's property was eaten up on prostitutes."[12] [13] Prostitution was well known in Israel, but it is never presented in a positive light in the Bible. Even in the case of Rahab, she is commended in spite of her occupation, not because of it. (Joshua 2:1-24; Hebrews 11:31; James 2:25) Prostitution is often associated with spiritual unfaithfulness. (Jeremiah 2:20; 3:1; Ezekiel 16:15-16; 23:5) In the New Testament, tax collectors and prostitutes are sometimes mentioned together. (Matthew 21:31-32) Within the Gentile world—and we must remember that the younger son had been in "a distant country"—prostitution was often connected with the worship of pagan gods. Was the older son hinting that beyond the moral sin of prostitution, his younger brother was also guilty of flirting with pagan deities? Or, as A. T. Robertson suggests, was he merely reflecting on what he would have done in similar circumstances?[14]

The parable doesn't tell us how the older son learned of his brother's involvement with prostitutes, or if it is even true. It may have been a baseless accusation since he probably had no contact with his brother and it is unlikely that he would have had any other source of information. Nevertheless, the accusation is never challenged. For the purpose of the parable it is presented as a fact.

The Elder Brother Syndrome

The attitude displayed by the older brother is common in our competitive world. We get the impression that this older son sees himself in competition with his younger brother. It's him against his brother, but this is more than just an inflated case of sibling rivalry.

I've coined the term "Elder Brother Syndrome" to describe this phenomenon. The elder brothers are the faithful people in society who obey the laws, pay their taxes, and contribute to community life in a myriad of ways. They often see their community involvement as a way of "giving back" for all the blessings they've enjoyed.

The same dynamic also thrives in many local churches. The elder brothers (whether male or female) pay the bills, lead church programs, attend worship faithfully, pray, sing the songs, and participate in clean-up days around the church. In short, they keep the doors open. They often get little or no recognition for tithing or for anything else that they do. In fact, after serving a term as a church officer they may not receive so much as a thank you note. But still, they are the backbone of the church. Without them, the church wouldn't be able to function.

On the other hand, every church has its prodigals. These are the people who tend to drift in and out of the church as needs in their lives present themselves. They might even have connections with any number of churches. Whenever a personal problem arises such as a utility bill they can't pay, an empty gas tank in their car, or a family matter that has escalated out of control, they'll show up at the church seeking help. And because of the faithfulness of the elder brothers, the church always seems to be there for them.

The Elder Brother Syndrome is that smug attitude, often unspoken, that says, *"Without people like me you wouldn't even have a place to go every time you get into trouble!"*

Every pastor has dealt with this issue at one time or another. There are people in every community who have never expressed any interest in the church or in living a Christian life, yet who have no qualms about coming to the church if they need something. And so the church distributes food, clothing, and gas vouchers, all in the hopeful expectation that the love of Jesus might make a positive impact in these people's lives. But rarely will someone who has received assistance actually attend a worship service.

The Elder Brother Syndrome is rooted in self-righteousness and cynicism. It identifies with the Pharisees and teachers of the law more than with the compassion of Jesus. (Luke 15:2) Most of all, those who possess it might silently resent the fact that they have never received the just recognition they feel they deserve. They feel taken for granted.

In a sense, they're right. In a healthy church we should always recognize and appreciate the accomplishments of others. In 1 Corinthians 16, Paul speaks of how the household of Stephanas "devoted themselves to the service of the Lord's people." He then speaks of how he had been blessed by men like Stephanas, Fortunatus and Achaicus. "Such men deserve recognition" he says. (1 Corinthians 16:18) Ideally, we would always "be devoted to one another in love" and to "honor one another above ourselves." (Romans 12:10)

Still, there's a critically important factor that we dare not overlook: *that service to the Lord is its own reward.* Consider another parable that Jesus told. In the Parable of the Workers in the Vineyard (Matthew 20:1-16), a landowner needs day laborers to work in his vineyard. He goes down to the community square at 6:00 in the morning and finds people who are willing to work the entire day for a denarius, the commonly expected wage for a day's employment. Later, at 9:00, he discovers that more workers are needed, so he returns to the community square and hires additional help. This time, however, he doesn't promise them a full denarius. He merely says that he will pay them "whatever is right." So they agree to come, not expecting to receive a full day's wage. They probably thought that receiving "whatever is right" would mean their pay would be prorated for the day.

The same thing happens at 12:00 noon, 3:00 in the afternoon, and finally as late as 5:00. Quitting time would typically be at 6:00. So at the end of the day, some of the workers had worked a full 12 hours, some only one hour, and others everything in between.

When it came time to pay the workers, the landowner called those who had worked only one hour to come in first, and he paid them a full denarius. In fact, everyone received a full denarius for the day's labor, regardless of how many hours they worked. Needless to say, those who had worked all day started to grumble, thinking that they deserved a bonus for their service. "These men who were hired last worked only one hour," they said, "and you have made them equal to us who have borne the burden of the work and the heat of the day." (Matthew 20:12)

Their situation wasn't so different from the older brother in the Parable of the Prodigal Son. They felt demeaned because others who had done far less work received equal compensation. They, too, suffered from a form of Elder Brother Syndrome. They felt entitled to receive more than they did and resented the father for offering his grace to those who didn't really deserve it. But they failed to understand that that they, themselves, didn't deserve grace any more than the other workers did. Besides, if you can earn it, then whatever it is, it isn't grace! (Romans 11:16)

The Parable of the Workers in the Vineyard ends with the landowner asking, "Don't I have the right to do what I want with my own money? Or are you envious because I am generous?" (Matthew

20:15) In the Parable of the Prodigal Son the same question applies. The father has the right to do whatever he wishes with his own money. And yes, the older son is clearly envious because of the generosity bestowed upon his younger brother.

The Older Son as Prodigal

When the Pharisees and the teachers of the law first heard Jesus tell this story, their sympathies would clearly have been with the older son. After all, he was certainly more moral than the wayward younger son. Perhaps they even saw themselves in the character of the older son, for they too, kept the law and lived exemplary lives.

Unlike the younger son, the older son never moved away. He never went to a distant country. He never squandered his inheritance or slept with prostitutes. Nevertheless, he shared an ironic characteristic with his younger brother: *he sought to live his life on his own terms, using his father's resources.* Both sons used their father as a means of securing their own self-centered desires. William Richardson explains:

> His goodness was a means to an end. He was obedient, but for the wrong reason. He saw his obedience as having bound his father to him—as having placed his father under some kind of obligation . . . Thus, out of his attempt to make his relationship with his father a matter of merit and reward, the other brother showed his heart to be as much out of tune with the father's as was that of the brother who took his father's patrimony and move to a far country.[15]

In short, the older son demonstrates the sense of entitlement that good, moral, decent people often feel. Misunderstanding the nature of grace, he felt he had earned a reward based on his good behavior and deeds. In essence, even God stood in his debt. And yet, at one point God asked Job, "Who has a claim against me that I must pay? Everything under heaven belongs to me." (Job 41:11) And later the Apostle Paul asks, "Who has ever given to God, that God should repay them?" (Romans 11:35) Regardless of how upright we may be, God doesn't owe us anything. On the contrary, it is we who owe God everything.

Win-Lose or Win-Win?

The older son's attitude, then, reveals an important underlying problem. The father loved both sons equally and wanted both of them to have equal honor in the family in spite of whatever shortcomings there have been in the past. The older son, however, viewed the situation in a competitive way. If there was to be a winner, it required a loser. The possibility of a win-win scenario never crossed his mind. Therefore, he interpreted the restoration of his younger brother to the family as a threat. In his mind, the triumphant return of his younger brother had turned him into a loser. As Fred Craddock observes "Even in religion it is very difficult not to think Jews *or* Gentiles, poor *or* rich, saint *or* sinner, publican *or* Pharisee, older son *or* younger son. But God's love is both/and, not either/or."[16]

When the father welcomed his younger son back into the family, he sought a win-win solution. All he ever wanted was to enjoy the fellowship of both his sons. He never intended for the inclusion of one to mean the exclusion of the other. And he certainly never entertained any thoughts of choosing between his two sons.

In the same way, loving tax collectors and sinners doesn't rule out loving Pharisees and teachers of the law. (Luke 15:1-2) The golden verse of the Bible assures us that "God so loved *the world* that he gave his one and only Son." (John 3:16) For God to show his love to one person or ethnic group does not require that he must think less of another. Even when God chose Israel to be his chosen people, he had the entire world in mind for redemption. And when God included the Gentiles in the plan of salvation, he never rejected Israel in the process. (Romans 11:1-24)[17] God created a win-win solution.

But not everyone will see it that way. New people coming into God's community can create a lot of unrest in the minds of older, more established people. What can the father say that would possibly change their minds?

Discussion

1. How would you feel if everyone in your family had received an invitation to a key family event except you? Which statement would best summarize your feelings? A) "I wasn't really forgotten. My invitation must have been lost in the mail."; B) "With so many things on the organizers' mind, I can overlook the obvious omission of my name on the guest list."; C) "I'm deeply hurt and it will take a while to get over this."
2. Do you think the older son was rude to vent his anger so freely?
3. Do you think the father was remiss by never recognizing his older son's faithful service in a tangible way?

4. The author says that "Service to the Lord is its own reward." Still, how does your church say thank you to those who have rendered faithful service?
5. If you had been the father, how would you have responded to your older son's outburst?
6. Since the community apparently was invited to the celebration, what role, if any, do you think "keeping up a good appearance" played in the father hosting this party?
7. Have you ever eaten goat meat? What "exotic meats" have you tried?
8. How did the older son know about his younger brother's involvement with prostitutes? Or did he?
9. Have you ever felt any of the symptoms of "Elder Brother Syndrome?" Explain.
10. The older brother believed he was entitled to a place in his father's house because of his good life. Does emphasizing grace demean the value of good works? (compare Ephesians 2:8-9 with James 2:24)
11. Did you have a competitive relationship with a brother or sister while growing up? In the end, did either of you "win?"

Chapter 11

The Result of Reconciliation

(Luke 15:31-32)

When we last left the older son he was angry, freely expressing his displeasure with his father for perhaps the first time in his life. In contrast to his father, he had completely cut his younger brother out of his life. If he had his way, his younger brother would be sent packing. Or at the very least, he might be accepted back only on a probationary basis. The father now tries to explain why the celebration is so important.

We must remember that Luke 15 consists of three parables told under the general theme of "lost and found." The first two parables speak of the joy that comes when that which is lost is found. But the direction of the third parable takes a dramatic turn. To rejoice over a lost sheep or coin is one thing. But not everyone rejoices when it is a lost human being that is found.

That's the major distinction that separates the Parable of the Prodigal Son from the first two parables. The result of being found, or in this case being reconciled, should be cause for great rejoicing.

And just as a lost sheep is restored to the flock and a lost coin is restored to the purse, so a lost son should be restored to his family. Tragically, as this story comes to a close we find the older son refusing to accept his younger brother back into the family. The result of reconciliation is often a mixed bag. It is joy for the lost sinner who has come home, but it can also reveal a refusal of God's children to be reconciled with each other. The final two verses of the story give a final demonstration of the father's heart in this matter.

My Son

> "My son," the father said, "you are always with me, and everything I have is yours. But we had to celebrate and be glad, because this brother of yours was dead and is alive again; he was lost and is found." (Luke 15:31-32)

It would be easy to skip over the words "My son" as the father begins his reply and yet these words are in the emphatic position, stressing the older son's legal right of inheritance.[1] We must remember that the older son had refused admit that he even had a younger brother any longer, preferring to call him "this son of yours." (Luke 15:30) But we now see the father's love extending to *both* of his sons. The same status and privileges of sonship that have been restored to the younger son have always belonged to the older son. In short, the father has *two* sons. Despite the older son's feelings to the contrary, to welcome one does not diminish the other in the father's eyes. So, the father begins by addressing the older brother as "my son," affirming both his love for him and his place in the family.

Always With Me

In the last chapter I suggested that service to the Lord contains its own reward. The father never denies that his older son has worked faithfully for him for the past number of years, although he will take issue with his older son describing his role in the family as "slavish." (Luke 15:29) "You are always with me," he says. (Luke 15:31) In other words, "You've always been with me, you're with me now, and I anticipate that you will always be with me in the future."[2] Just think of the heartache the older son has been spared! His younger brother has suffered the full consequences of a life of sin: physically, morally, socially, economically, and spiritually. He has gone through the agony of being separated from his father. Seeking his freedom, he has discovered how enslaving sin can become.

In contrast, the older son has always stayed home. While his younger brother experienced cold, hunger, loneliness and the threat of catching a sexually transmitted disease out in the distant country, the older brother has always had plenty to eat, a warm bed to sleep in at night, and most importantly, the love of his father.

Until the celebration of the prodigal's return took place, we only had a vague hint that there was any tension between the older son and his father. But now we know better. The older son's resentment is not based on finances, however. In fact, his younger brother's original demand for his share of the inheritance had cost him nothing. Indeed, when the father divided his estate between them, the elder son also received his share at the same time. (Luke 15:12)

Since this is a story created by Jesus, we probably shouldn't speculate too much further than that. Jesus never tells us what the older son thought of the original financial arrangement or of his father's wisdom in allowing it. Still, the older son now clearly resents both his younger brother and his father. We get the impression that perhaps the father is surprised by his older son's anger. Perhaps he's had no idea of the resentment that has been brewing over the years. Everything reaches a boiling point when the older son sees the celebration at his brother's return.

Everything I Have is Yours

The father points out to his older son that "everything I have is yours." (Luke 15:31) A better understanding is "everything I have has always been yours."[3] Although the older son had received his share of the inheritance at the same time that the younger son did, the father still exercised the usufruct of it. Just as the younger son was free to spend it in any way he chose, so the older son also enjoyed that same right. Therefore, he was in error when he complained that "You never gave me even a young goat so I could celebrate with my friends." (Luke 15:29) The truth of the matter is that he already enjoyed everything his father had to give. He could have had a BBQ with goat meat (or even beef!) in the company of his friends any time he wanted. Like many people who have been richly blessed, he failed to recognize, appreciate, or appropriate the full extent of his blessing.

But in a larger sense, are we to assume that when the father said *"everything* I have is yours," he was referring only to his material wealth? Surely included in the wealth was something that was beyond price: his legacy of unconditional love! The father did not withhold anything from either of his two sons.

We Had to Celebrate

The father continues by saying, "We had to celebrate . . ." (Luke 15:32) Some translations unnecessarily soften this phrase by rendering it "It was right" (New King James Version) or "It was fitting" (Revised Standard Version), or even "There was a good reason" (Knox). The Greek word *edei* shows an imperfect imperative. In other words, the celebration was an absolute necessity.[4] Perhaps even more revealing is that the imperfect tense shows continued action. The joy of the younger son's return was not to conclude when the musicians and dancers had gone home, or after the leftovers had all been eaten. The joy was expected to continue on and into the future. They must never forget the reason behind the celebration.

This Brother of Yours

Why must the joy continue? The father says it's because of the older son's continuing relationship with "this brother of yours." (Luke 15:32) Earlier the older son had referred to his younger brother as "this son of yours" in an attempt to distance himself from him. (Luke 15:30) The father grasped the subtlety behind his son's choice of words. Without directly challenging them, however, the father now calls his younger son "this brother of yours."

The language here is significant. The action of the younger son had broken the family, but now the older son's action is equally heartbreaking. As Francois Bovon has observed, the younger son left the father by going away, while the older son left him from the inside.[5] But in either case, they had both "left home." And when they distanced themselves from their father they also distanced themselves from the rest of his family.

Living in Community

The actions of both sons show a misunderstanding of what it means to live in community. In America, one of our greatest values is our independence, both nationally and individually. Herbert Hoover coined the phrase "rugged individualism" to describe the view that nearly everyone has the ability to succeed socially and economically on their own, with minimal assistance from others.[6] Self-reliance is the key. And so we admire the self-made person who is able to pull himself up by his own bootstraps.

Julie Gorman notes, "Our heroes are the solo survivors, the prima donnas, the Lone Rangers, and the self-sufficient entrepreneurs who made it to the top by climbing over others."[7] The many so-called "reality" television programs that are so popular in our day attest to this rugged "last man standing" value. The individual is maximized, while the value of the group becomes secondary.

Gorman continues by observing that our culture is becoming more and more *me* oriented, where the larger group is viewed as existing to serve the interests of the individual. The primary concern is not what's in the best interest of others, but rather each individual. In other words, "I will relate to you if it does something for me."[8] This is not to say that individuals won't join groups. However, they often will choose to participate on *their* terms, not on the terms of the group and only so long as they feel they are deriving some personal benefit from their involvement. Altruistic service is not the prime consideration for many people; the common good easily becomes subordinate to personal self-interest.

Such an attitude is contrary to New Testament teaching, however. The Apostle Paul writes, "Now to each one the manifestation of the Spirit is given for the common good." (1 Corinthians 12:7) While God's gifts are given to individuals, they are given for the benefit of the community as a whole. Later, Paul will also write, "In humility value others above yourselves, not looking to your own interests but each of you to the interests of the others." (Philippians 2:3b-4) Rick Warren was right when he began his bestselling book *The Purpose Driven Life* with the words, "It's not about you."[9]

It is significant that the experience of the earliest Christians always took place within the context of community.[10] Conversion itself was often experienced within the framework of a household. (Luke 19:9; John 4:53; Acts 10:2; 11:14; 16:15, 31-34; 18:8; 1 Corinthians 1:16; 16:15) It is not surprising, therefore, that Paul would write, "You are no longer foreigners and strangers, but fellow citizens with God's people and also members of God's household." (Ephesians 2:19) God's people are connected together as a family. As I. Howard Marshall notes, "To be a Christian was to be a member of the church. What matters for Luke is that Christians come together and share in the common life of the church—in fellowship, in prayer and in mission."[11]

Sadly, neither of the sons in the parable appreciated their community connection. They both sought self-fulfillment on their own terms; both were estranged from their father and family as a result. The younger son did it by leaving home for a distant country, while the older son did it by being so righteously moral that he expected everyone, including his father, to be indebted to him. Both were willing to sacrifice their connection with the family in pursuit of their own individual agendas.

> Sadly, neither of the two sons in the parable appreciated their community connection. They both sought self-fulfillment on their own terms; both were estranged from their father and family as a result.

Dead and Lost; Alive and Found

Despite his love for his younger son, the father has no delusions as to the current state of affairs. Earlier, upon his son's return, the father justified the celebration to his servants by saying, "For this son of mine was dead and is alive again; he was lost and is found." (Luke 15:24) Now as he speaks to his older son he uses essentially the same words.[12] (Luke 15:32)

Within Judaism there was a ceremony found in the Talmud whereby a father could formally disown a child. The father would take a large ceramic pot and fill it with burnt corn, beans, and raisins. He would then go outside of his house, publicly break the pot and proclaim "My son is cut off from his people." In so doing he "divested" himself of everything pertaining to his son. Such a move not only signaled the complete break of a relationship, it also provided legal protection for the father against any future actions by his son. In addition, the community as a whole would support the father's divestiture by shunning his wayward son should they ever see him again. No one would ever speak to him, let alone give him a job.[13]

Interestingly, there was also a ceremony for "reinvesting" a son should the two become reconciled.[14] Since there is no mention of the father in this parable taking advantage of such legal and social protection, it demonstrates that his love for his son remained steadfast in spite of the fact that his son was both "dead" and "lost." As such, he stands in contrast to what many other fathers would have done. Since apparently no "divesting" ceremony was performed, no "reinvesting" ceremony was warranted. All that was necessary was to celebrate his younger son's return.

Cliffhanger

As the Parable of the Prodigal Son ends, the music is still playing and people are still dancing in celebration. Nevertheless, the older son remains outside of the house, refusing to go in, while his father continues to plead with him. The father's purpose remains unchanged: *he still seeks the restoration of relationship with all of his children, and for his children to live in harmony with each other.*

Those who like stories where all the loose ends of the plot are neatly resolved will certainly be disappointed with this ending. So many questions are left unanswered! Did the father finally convince his older son to join the party or did he remain outside? Did the son acquiesce, just as he had always done, even though his heart wasn't in it? How long did the father plead with him? Did he ever give up? Certainly the father and his older son would have been missed at the celebration. What did the people inside think about their absence, even if only for a short time?

By ending this parable so abruptly, Jesus knew his listeners would doubtless ask questions such as these. In addition, by drawing them into the story he invited them to ponder where they might find themselves in it.

We must remember that the original audience was a mixed crowd, consisting of tax collectors, "sinners," Pharisees and teachers of the law. (Luke 15:1-2) They were the classic "outsiders" and "insiders" of Jewish society. Perhaps the tax collectors and "sinners" found sympathy with the younger son, who wandered far away from his roots, but who later discovered that he still had a father who would forgive him if he would only come home. Perhaps they were encouraged to come home to the Lord in repentance, much like the tax collector in another parable that Jesus told, who stood off at a distance, head bowed down, beating his chest, and crying "God, have mercy on me, a sinner." (Luke 18:9-13)

The Pharisees and the teachers of the law, on the other hand, would have been more problematic. On several occasions Jesus accused these religious leaders of being blind. (Matthew 15:12-14; 23:16, 19, 26; John 9:39-41) Were they able to see themselves as the self-righteous older brother who also needed to be reconciled with his father? Or would they have still commended him for his faithful, law abiding service? Perhaps they would have even condemned the father for siding with sinners![15] But then, as we've noted, there are really two prodigals in this story. One realized his lost condition and came home. Who can say what happened to the other?

What Matters Most

In the end, what matters most is the place in which you find yourself within Jesus' story. Perhaps you identify with the younger son and know what it's like to make bad decisions in life—decisions that often bring dire consequences. You might even question whether or not you can come home again after squandering so much and hurting so many people who were once close to you. You might wonder, "Is reconciliation with my family or friends even possible? And where is God in all of this? How many times can I fail God and still expect him to take me back?"

If this describes you, the parable offers a unique glimpse of a heavenly father who not only will take you back, but who is actively searching for you! It serves as a reminder that "The Lord is gracious and compassionate, slow to anger and rich in love. The Lord is good to all; he has compassion on all he has made." (Psalm 145:8-9)

But with this assurance also comes a warning. True forgiveness does not mean pretending that an offense never occurred. On the contrary, where there is no grievance there is no need of forgiveness. The younger son discovered that any reconciliation with his father demanded a reorientation of his life. In short, he had to change his ways if he was going to once again enjoy the full benefits of his father, family and friends.

Perhaps, however, you relate more to the older son in this story. Perhaps you're a good person who keeps the law, pays your taxes, and who is maybe even active in your church. All these things are commendable, of course. But deep down you also find yourself resenting those who seem to have a harder time with life than you do. You wonder, "Why can't they pay their bills? Why can't they keep their commitments or hold down a job? Why do problems always seem to surround them? Why can't they make better decisions?"

If this describes you, then this parable might lead you to identify areas of weakness in your own life. The inherent danger of self-satisfaction is one of the reasons why Jesus said it was easier for a camel to go through the eye of a needle than for a rich man to enter into the kingdom of God. (Matthew 19:24) You might begin to think that you've got everything all figured out. You might even want to commend yourself for being such an upstanding person, just like the older son did in Jesus' story.

It's all a matter of the heart, however. Such an attitude demeans grace because deep down you have a feeling of entitlement—that God owes you something because of your goodness. You deserve to be rewarded. Still, as the angel instructed John to write concerning the church at Laodicea, "You say, 'I am rich; I have acquired wealth and do not need a thing.' But you do not realize that you are wretched, pitiful, poor, blind and naked." (Revelation 3:17) Remember that both the younger and older sons were prodigals in Jesus' story.

But there's one last major character in Jesus' story. At the risk of sounding too arrogant, perhaps you relate most to the father. Maybe you're at your wits' end raising teenagers or watching the choices being made by your friends or adult children. You want to cry out, "How can they do such things?" And just as the father in the story ended up financing his younger son's excursion into "wine, women and song," maybe you've bailed out your kids following poor choices that they've made. Remember that the primary sin of the younger son was that he wanted to live his life on his own terms, apart from his father, while utilizing his father's resources.

The concept of "tough love" is admittedly difficult for many parents.[16] At its core is the idea that long term benefits can be gained when loved ones are not shielded from the consequences of their actions. The hope is that inappropriate behavior will change in the face of a firm, consistent and loving response by those surrounding them. But it can be difficult. That's why they call it *tough* love.

Still, the father in Jesus' story never gives up and never stops hoping. Day by day he goes out in search of his son, hoping against all hope that he will one day return. If that describes your relationship with a friend or one of your children, then my advice is that you show your compassion by standing firm in what you know is right. In addition, pray that God will bring the right people and influences into their lives while they are away. For just as you haven't stopped loving them, God hasn't either.

In the end, that's the greatest lesson of the Parable of the Prodigal Son. We have a loving father who is still waiting for us to come home and to live in harmony with him and with the rest of his family. Amen.

Discussion

1. Tommy Smothers used to chide his younger brother Dick by saying, "Mom always did like you best." Was there a favorite in your family while growing up? If so, how did it affect everyone else?
2. The resentment the older son had for his father had evidently been brewing for some time. Why do you suppose he felt so alienated?
3. The older son received his share of the inheritance at the same time his younger brother did. How free do you think he really was to spend it as he wished? What constraints might there have been?
4. Do you think people are more "me oriented" today than they were a generation ago? Why or why not?
5. Even though the New Testament stresses the role of community in the Christian life, what reasons might some believers give for living their lives apart from a church?
6. How do the people of your church generally respond when a member who's been gone for a long time suddenly returns?
7. Of the three major characters in this parable, which one do you identify with the most—the younger son, the older son, or the father? Explain.

Chapter 12

Morals to the Stories

Depending upon how we count them, Jesus told as many as 65 parables that have been recorded for us in the gospels. The two parables in this study are undoubtedly the best known of them all. While most of Jesus' recorded parables tend to be short, the Parables of the Good Samaritan and the Prodigal Son have six and 21 verses respectively, making them among the longest of Jesus' parables. In addition, both parables have a fairly extensive context that is provided. The Parable of the Good Samaritan is introduced by Jesus' encounter with a lawyer, while the Parable of the Prodigal Son parable is preceded by the grumbling of Pharisees and teachers of the law, and by the Parables of the Lost Sheep and the Lost Coin. The result is that the characters in the two parables we've studied are a little more developed than in most other parables and are therefore more memorable.

Perhaps that's why we love these two stories so much. We understand them. They speak of circumstances we all encounter in everyday life, asking us to find ourselves within them. Who among us hasn't been faced with a legitimate need and yet felt we had good reason for doing nothing? We've all been priests and

Levites. And who hasn't determined at one time or another to go his (or her) own way in life? We've all been prodigals, whether like the younger or older son. These two parables speak to our human condition like no other.

Basic Similarities

The Parables of the Good Samaritan and Prodigal Son have a number of similarities. First, they are both found only in the Gospel of Luke. Since the Gospel of John doesn't contain any of Jesus' parables, we wouldn't expect to find then there, but Matthew and Mark are different. Called *synoptic gospels,* Mathew, Mark and Luke are all seen "through the same eyes." That is, they tell the story of Jesus from roughly the same vantage point. Each writer, under the guidance of the Holy Spirit, crafted his gospel by his choice of words and by what he chose to include and exclude. For whatever reason, neither Matthew nor Mark chose to include these two popular parables in their gospel accounts.

Another point in common is that both stories were originally told to an antagonistic audience. The Parable Good Samaritan was told to a lawyer who "stood up to test Jesus." (Luke 10:25) The Parable of the Prodigal Son was told to Pharisees and teachers of the law who condemned Jesus for eating with tax collectors and sinners. (Luke 15:1-2) In both cases Jesus handled those who opposed him with courtesy and respect, while at the same time standing up to them.[1]

Both parables also share a similar structure. The most obvious structural similarity is the focus on three major characters. The Good Samaritan story features a man who falls among robbers, a priest and Levite (who are treated as a single unit) and a Samaritan.

The Parable of the Prodigal Son focuses on the father and his two sons.

In addition, both parables share a similar *chiasm*, or orderly pattern. The pattern employed is an "inverted parallelism," where a series of dynamics is introduced in the first half of the story, only to be found again in reverse order in the second half. In the Parable of the Good Samaritan the chiasm looks like this:[2]

1) a man falls among thieves and suffers great loss
   2) a priest (riding an animal?) passes by on the other side of the road
      3) a Levite passes by on the other side of the road
         4) a Samaritan sees the man and has compassion
      3') the Samaritan provides first aid
   2') the Samaritan puts the man on his own animal and takes him to an inn
1') the Samaritan pays the bill until the man is restored

In the example above, each number roughly corresponds to its opposite. (1 corresponds to 1'; 2 corresponds to 2', etc.). In this instance the number 4 has no corresponding counterpoint. The Parable of the Prodigal Son is lengthier, yet follows the same basic "inverted parallel" chiastic pattern. It looks like this:[3]

1) a son is lost—"Give me my share"
   2) goods wasted
      3) everything is lost—he spends everything and is in want
         4) sin—a Jew feeding pigs
            5) rejection—"no one gave him anything"
               6) a change of mind—"he came to himself"

6') repentance—"I will go to my father"
5') acceptance—"his father ran and kissed him"
4') great repentance—"not worthy to be called your son"
3') everything is regained—robe, ring, shoes
2') goods used in joyful celebration
1') a son is found—son was dead, but now alive

While these chiastic patterns are interesting and help us to appreciate the orderliness of scripture, it's important not to force a preconceived structure upon what we read in the Bible. In an attempt to make things fit a pattern, it's easy to place too much of an emphasis on minor details or to overlook something that's truly important. Note, for example, that the older son never appears in the chiasm of the Parable of Prodigal Son and yet he is a major character in the story.

Someone once observed that "It's very easy to play the violin poorly." In the same way, it is very easy to impose our ideas upon a passage rather than allowing it to speak for itself. The danger, of course, is that we might end up "playing the Bible poorly." So while studying chiastic patterns can be fascinating and serves any number of useful purposes, we do not wish to push them too far. Still, the structural similarity between these two parables is striking.

The Theme of Salvation

In both parables we are introduced to characters who find themselves in dire situations. In the Parable of the Good Samaritan a man falls among robbers, is stripped, beaten and left for dead. In the Parable of the Prodigal Son, the younger son is also considered to be dead. He demands his share of the inheritance, blows it on "wine, women, and song," and is not only forced to tend pigs, but is reduced to eating pig slop. The older son in the parable is no less dead, for while he lives at home he is emotionally distant from his father. All three of these characters end up alone and isolated. Left on their own, there's little hope for any of them. In short, apart from the intervention from an outside source they face a very dim future.

While neither of these two stories is primarily about our eternal salvation, it's hard to overlook salvation's overtones in them.[4] As we've seen, many have said that the Good Samaritan typifies Jesus, but that seems to be a bit forced. Even though the Parable of the Good Samaritan was preceded by a question and answer session on how to inherit eternal life, the story was not told in response to that specific issue. Instead, the question posed was, "And who is my neighbor?" (Luke 10:29) To take a story about being a neighbor and turn it into a treatise on how Jesus saves pushes the story too far. Furthermore, in the Parable of the Prodigal Son there is no doctrine of atonement presented, causing some to believe the story is more about a backsliding Christian (that is, a Christian who is not living up to what he believes) than it is about someone who has never known Christ. I have taken the view that the primary message is about the joy that should exist when the lost are found. But in any case, it's pretty clear in the parable that you can always come home to the Father.

And so while neither of these two parables is specifically about salvation, it's hard to read them without seeing salvation's overtones. Jesus *does* save. And Jesus *is* merciful, just as the Good Samaritan was. God welcomes us home, just as the father welcomed both of his sons.

Like the wounded traveler or either of the father's two sons, we've all been in situations where, try as we might, we just can't escape our plight on our own. Marriages come to an end. Houses go into foreclosure. People file for bankruptcy. A misunderstanding drives a wedge between lifelong friends. A doctor says that it's time to consider hospice care. Perhaps you've felt like the wounded traveler—stripped, robbed, beaten and abandoned. Or like the son in a distant country, starving to death. Or even like the son who stayed at home, but whose heart was somehow still far away. And like the psalmist, you've wondered "Where does my help come from?" (Psalm 121:1)

Sometimes we hold on for dear life, fearing what the future might hold for us. We read that "neither death nor life, neither angels nor demons, neither the present nor the future, nor any powers, neither height nor depth, nor anything else in all creation, will be able to separate us from the love of God that is in Christ Jesus our Lord." (Romans 8:38-39) We come to understand that while a Christian may suffer many of the same pressures and drawbacks in life as anyone else, God's love is always there to empower and sustain us.

Still, our faith is more than simply a way to feel better about a bad situation. God's love also has practical aspects. From a practical standpoint, God can provide assistance from many different sources—from friends, relatives, counselors, or even from the government. One of the greatest ways in which God meets the needs of his people, however, is through his church. The Apostle Paul's experience serves as an example. Within the context of his own imprisonment and deprivations, he thanks the Philippian church for reviving their financial support for his ministry. And then he writes, "Do not be anxious about anything, but in everything, by prayer and petition, with thanksgiving, present your requests to God . . . And my God will meet all your needs according to the riches of his glory in Christ Jesus." (Philippians 4:6, 19) In other words, just as God had met Paul's needs (in this case, through the church), so God will also meet your needs as well. We dare not overlook the fact that Paul was writing to Christians who had banded together and who were living a covenanted life together in a local church, a church in which Paul was both known and connected. The church was the means by which God met Paul's needs.[5] Believers who are not associated with any local church are sadly separated from this simple means of both giving and receiving encouragement and support.

Our greatest need, of course, has to do with our eternal relationship with God—a relationship that begins in the here and now. Left on our own, we could never attain or enjoy fellowship with the Father. Again, to quote the Apostle Paul, "You see, at just the right time, when we were still powerless, Christ died for the ungodly . . . God demonstrates his own love for us in this: While we were still sinners, Christ died for us." (Romans 5:6, 8) Christ is the agent through whom spiritual wholeness is found. God took the initiative when we were stripped, beaten, robbed and left for dead. God looked out and saw us when we were still in a distant country, far from home, going our own way. Or even when we were at home (or at church?), going through all the right motions, but still somehow far away. Someone put it this way:

> If our greatest need had been information, God would have sent us an educator; If our greatest need had been technology, God would have sent us a scientist; If our greatest need had been money, God would have sent us an economist; If our greatest need had been pleasure, God would have sent us an entertainer; But our greatest need was forgiveness, so God sent us a Savior.[6]

D. H. Shearer

The Theme of Harmonious Relationships

Closely related to the theme of salvation is our relationship with other people. The Parable of the Prodigal Son demonstrates that we cannot be fully reconciled with God until we are also at peace with the rest of his children. Everyone who calls God his Father must also acknowledge every Christian to be his brother or sister.

The Parable of the Good Samaritan takes this issue even further. The Samaritan crosses ethnic and religious boundaries in order to assist a wounded traveler. Therefore, to be in a right relationship with God also involves treating people of all nationalities and faiths with loving respect. It allows for no double standard in the way we treat people. It is through such channels of love and respect that the gospel most easily travels. In short, the gospel calls us to "live at peace with everyone." (Romans 12:18) The "everyone" in this case includes Christians and non-Christians, friends and enemies, rich and poor. "Peacemakers who sow in peace raise a harvest of righteousness." (James 3:18)

The key to harmonious relationships is understanding that, appearances sometimes to the contrary, all of our interactions with other people are not linear as often supposed, but triangular.[7] A linear relationship involves only two parties and everything flows back and forth between them. A triangular relationship, however, always includes a third party. The Christian has been "clothed with Christ" in baptism. (Galatians 3:27) Christ is now a part of the equation and a silent partner in every relationship. As a Christian, you begin to see others as Christ sees them and his love and compassion begins to flow through you. In the case of the Good Samaritan, it meant crossing social and spiritual boundaries to be of assistance because that's what Christ would do. And for the two prodigal sons it meant they must be reconciled with each other before they could expect the full blessing of being reconciled with their father. Living in harmony with other people is central to both of these parables.

Of course, any relationship requires a certain amount of risk as both parables illustrate. Love freely extended is not always returned and is sometimes abused. Even the happiest of relationships will eventually include a degree of disappointment. In addition, no human relationship lasts forever. Couples who have enjoyed long, happy marriages inevitably suffer the pain of separation when one of the spouses dies. It goes with the territory, however. Are we to stop loving because love ultimately leaves us vulnerable? Will the fear of loss deprive us of the joy of love?

When the Good Samaritan helped the man who fell among thieves he put himself in a very vulnerable position. For all he knew the "victim" was faking and would turn on him as he rendered assistance. In the Parable of the Prodigal Son the father also made himself vulnerable. When he divided his inheritance between his two sons, he not only took a financial risk but also faced social embarrassment among his friends and neighbors. What's more, when his younger son finally returned there was no guarantee that the irresponsible behavior of the past wouldn't repeat itself. The father also risked further alienation with his older son when he hosted a celebratory BBQ.

When God sent his son he made himself vulnerable. At the cross we learned that God would rather die than to live apart from us. And yet, "We all, like sheep, have gone astray, each of us has turned to our own way; and the Lord has laid on him the iniquity of us all." (Isaiah 53:6) The Apostle Paul

> When God sent his son he made himself vulnerable. At the cross we learned that God would rather die than to live apart from us.

further expressed God's frustration and vulnerability when he quoted Isaiah 65:2, "All day long I have held out my hands to a disobedient and obstinate people." (Romans 10:21) A harmonious relationship always requires sound discernment and an element of risk, but the gospel makes it clear that it is well worth it in the end.

The Theme of Action

Finally, both of these parables are action-oriented. Jesus summarizes the point behind the Good Samaritan story with the words, "Go and do likewise." (Luke 10:37) It's not a story about proper attitudes or sound doctrine. Those themes can be found elsewhere in the Bible. Rather, putting your faith into practice is the dominant emphasis of this parable—even when it might make you uncomfortable or costs you something. In the case of the two prodigals, however, the father has an interesting role. On the one hand, he is a stable figure in the story. He goes nowhere, stays home and manages his estate. All throughout the story his sons know exactly where they can find him. And yet he is also seen as someone who is constantly taking the initiative. He sees his younger son while he is still far off, implying that he's been out looking for his return all along. When his older son stands outside the celebration and refuses to participate, the father again takes the initiative by seeking him out. So, notwithstanding his stationary position at home, the father is clearly a man of action.

But so are both of the sons. Of course, the younger son starts with a poor action. He demands his share of the inheritance moves away and squanders it, but he later "comes to himself" and travels home. If the only issue to him was poverty and hunger, he had other options than returning to his father. The father waited patiently, hoping against hope that someday he would come back, but the younger son had to act by taking the first step.

The older son also found himself in a position where he had to take action, although the story finishes without telling us the final outcome. Throughout the story he had performed his daily duties and behaved himself. In some ways he typifies someone who thinks he can be justified by the works of the law. (Romans 3:28; Galatians 2:16) He had a sense of entitlement because of his goodness. He failed to understand that he, too, was trying to live life on his own terms. He was alienated from his father and needed his father's grace every bit as much as his younger brother. Jesus finished the story with the older son standing outside, refusing to go in. Perhaps this was the Lord's way of saying, "The choice is now yours. What will you do?"

In the end, we realize that our Christian faith is not merely a matter of believing or saying all the right things. True faith, if it is genuine, means being reconciled with God through Jesus Christ and living in harmony with other people. Such a relationship is dynamic and must be lived out with each passing day. As James wrote, "In the same way, faith by itself, if it is not accompanied by action, is dead." (James 2:17)

So each of us must ask, "Where do I find myself in these two parables? Am I a neighbor? Or am I a ne'er-do-well?"

Discussion

1. What is it about the Parables of the Good Samaritan and the Prodigal Son that makes them so loved?
2. What other well-known parables that Jesus told come to mind? Do they bear any resemblance to the two parables we've studied?

3. Since both parables were told to an antagonistic audience, what can we learn from Jesus' example that might help us to interact with the negative people that we encounter?
4. Chiastic patterns have been found all throughout the Bible. What do you think about them? Are they fascinating to you? Are they the product of a theologian's imagination? Somewhere in between?
5. Have you ever found yourself in the middle of a bad situation that you just couldn't fix? What finally happened? What "saved" you?
6. Looking back with 20-20 hindsight, what means has God used in the past to meet your physical, emotional and spiritual needs?
7. Is there someone right now with whom you need to be reconciled? What steps might you take?
8. What opportunities has God given you to draw closer to him?

Endnotes

Chapter 1: The Power of Parables

[1] Aristotle, *The Art of Rhetoric*, c. 367-322 BC, Book II, Chapter 20. Aristotle equated parables with fables. Most modern interpreters, however, make a distinction between the two, holding that fables might anthropomorphize animals, plants, inanimate objects and forces of nature while parables do not.

[2] Other examples of parables in the Old Testament include 1 Kings 20:39-42; Isaiah 5:1-7; 28:21-29; Ezekiel 17:1-24; 19:1-14; 20:45-49; 24:3-14.

[3] As cited by Klyne R. Snodgrass, "Parable," *Dictionary of Jesus and the Gospels* (Joel B. Green, Scot McKnight, I Howard Marshall, eds.; Downers: Grove: InterVarsity Press, 1992), 593-594. Snodgrass observes that some scholars find this fourfold classification to be unworkable on technical grounds, but I believe it serves us well for the purpose of this study.

[4] Other examples of this type of parable can be found in Matthew 15:10-20; Mark 7:17; Luke 5:36-39.

[5] The NIV renders *parabolē* as "in a manner of speaking" in this verse. Older NIV editions translate it as "figuratively speaking."

[6] Delling prefers thinking of fulfillment in terms of a text finding its completion. Gerhard Delling, *"Plēroō," Theological Dictionary of the New Testament*, (Vol. 6.; Gerhard Kittel and Gerhard Friedrich, eds.,

transl. Geoffrey Bromiley; Grand Rapids: Eerdmans, 1968), 295. Delling's view implies a living dynamism within the text, as it grows from its incomplete inception to its completed wholeness.

[7] Called by theologians *Sitz im Leben,* German for "setting in life."

[8] Richard A. Jenson, *Thinking in Story: Preaching in a Post-literate Age* (Lima, OH: CSS Publishing, 1993), 28.

[9] This is an example of Jesus engaging in hyperbole for the purpose of emphasis. There are obviously smaller seeds than mustard seeds in the world, but these were the smallest seeds commonly planted in the area at the time.

[10] Again, Jesus uses hyperbole. There are larger plants that grow in gardens, but the contrast between the small seed and the large, mature plant should not be overlooked.

[11] Isaiah 6:9-10

Chapter 2: Approaching the Parable of the Good Samaritan

[1] In response, the Samaritans believed that they and not the Jews were the true heirs of orthodoxy. When the center of national worship was moved from Gerizim to Shiloh and eventually to Jerusalem, the Samaritans interpreted it as the beginning of Israel's apostasy. The Samaritans faithfully held to the original Gerizim location, near Shechem. In addition, they believed the Pentateuch alone was authoritative, without the addition of the prophets. Although the Samaritans' views were not always homogeneous, they believed that they had held fast to the original founding and ideals of Israel, while the Jews had accepted numerous new and unauthorized tenents. Still, they did not regard themselves as a remnant of the old kingdom of Israel, but rather as a separate expression of God's people existing alongside of it. The animosity between Jews and Samaritans flowed both ways. H. G. M. Williamson, "Samaritans," *Dictionary of Jesus*

and the Gospels (Joel B. Green and Scot McKnight, eds.; Downers Grove, Ill: InterVarsity, 1992), 724-728.

[2] David A. Wallace, "Allegory," *Baker Dictionary of Theology* (Everett F. Harrison, ed.; Grand Rapids: Baker, 1960), 37.

[3] Craig Blomberg, *Preaching the Parables: From Responsible Interpretation to Powerful Proclamation* (Grand Rapids: Baker Academic, 2004), 58.

[4] Augustine, *The Question of the Gospels*, II, 19.

[5] John Newton, "How Kind the Good Samaritan," *Olney Hymns* (London: W. Oliver, 1779), No. 99. The meter is 8888, which, if the last two lines are repeated, accommodates the hymn tune St. Catherine (commonly associated with "Faith of Our Fathers").

[6] John Calvin, *Commentary on Matthew, Mark and Luke*, (Vol. 3; trans. William Pringle; Grand Rapids: Baker, reprint 2009), 63. John Calvin's disdain for interpreting parables allegorically placed him in the minority of his day's Biblical interpreters.

[7] Cited by Alger Fitch, *Preaching Christ* (Joplin, MO: College Press, 1992), 98.

Chapter 3: The Attorney and His Agenda

[1] William F. Arndt and F. Wilber Gingrich, *A Greek-English Lexicon of the New Testament and other Early Christian Literature* (4th ed., Chicago: University of Chicago Press, 1952), *"eidon,"* 219.

[2] It is important to remember that the lawyer was concerned about "doing," because at the end of the parable Jesus will tell him to "Go and *do* likewise." Fred B. Craddock, *Luke* (Interpretation: A Bible Commentary for Preaching and Teaching; Louisville: John Knox, 1990), 149-150.

[3] R.C.H. Lenski, *The Interpretation of St. Luke's Gospel* (Minneapolis: Augsburg, 1946), 598.

4   Mark C. Black, *Luke* (College Press NIV Commentary; Joplin, MO: College Press, 1996), 215. Black observes that "It is tempting to interpret [the aspects of heart, soul, strength and mind] in modern terms such as the emotional, the spiritual, the physical, and the intellectual; however the intent is simply to love God with all of one's being."

5   W. E. Vine, *An Expository Dictionary of New Testament Words* (Vol. 3., Old Tappan, NJ: Revell, 1940), "Mind, *dianoia*," 69.

6   George A. F. Knight, *Leviticus* (Daily Bible Study Series; Louisville: Westminster John Knox, 1981), 121.

7   "In everything do to others what you would have them do to you, for this sums up the Law and the Prophets." (Matthew 7:12)

8   Thomas Campbell observed, "This wretched, naked, half-murdered poor creature was their *neighbor*; that is, their fellow-creature, made in the same divine image with themselves, and therefore worthy of their sympathy and assistance. Our blessed Savior, by this example, teaches us that every man is our neighbor, no matter how poor, fallen, and wretched he may be; because he is our fellow creature, he is our neighbor, and we must *love him as ourself*." (Italics in the original). Thomas Campbell, "Farewell Discourse of Elder Thos. Campbell," *Millennial Harbinger* (March, 1854), 136.

9   Love fulfills the law. See Romans 13:8-10; Galatians 5:14; James 2:8.

10 Craddock, 150.

11 Craddock, 150.

12 Karl Barth, *Church Dogmatics* (Vol.1; Edinburgh: T. and T. Clark, 1956), 417.

13 William Barclay, *The Gospel of Luke* (The Daily Study Bible Series, Rev. Ed.; Philadelphia: Westminster, 1975), 140.

14 Cited by Kenny Boles, *New Testament Words: Chosen* (http://occ.edu.words/; downloaded September 18, 2011.)

Chapter 4: Crime and Compassion

[1] Contra Alfred Plummer, *The Gospel According to St. Luke* (New York: Scribner's, 1925), 285-286. Plummer argues that nowhere else does Jesus speak of a specific priest or Levite in a disparaging way, so it would be out of character for him to create a story placing one in a bad light. Adam Clarke also suggests that had this story been understood as a mere parable the lawyer would certainly have objected that no such case ever existed. Clarke therefore assumes that Jesus was referring to an actual event of which the lawyer was familiar. Adam Clarke, *Adam Clarke's Commentary on the Bible* (Vol. 5, New York: Abingdon, n.d.), 43.

[2] As Luke crafts his gospel account of Jesus he places an episode with Mary and Martha immediately following the Parable of the Good Samaritan, as if to provide balance. (Luke 10:38-42) If one of the messages of the Good Samaritan is "Go and do," then the message behind the Mary and Martha episode is "Sit down and listen." As Craddock observes, "There is a time to go and do; there is a time to listen and reflect. Knowing which and when is a matter of spiritual discernment." Fred Craddock, *Luke* (Interpretation: A Bible Commentary for Preaching and Teaching; Louisville: John Knox, 1990), 149, 152.

[3] Marcus Borg, in his book *Reading the Bible Again for the First Time*, takes a different angle than I do. When he speaks of reading the Bible again, he means to do so through what he calls new "lenses," utilizing a non-literal approach both in terms of the Bible's historicity and what accurately expresses God's will. For my part, I simply mean to cast aside preconceived notions and approach the sacred text as those who first heard it might have understood it. See Marcus Borg, *Reading the Bible Again for the First Time* (San Francisco: Harper, 2001), 3-6.

[4] Cited by J. W. McGarvey and Philip Y. Pendleton, *Fourfold Gospel* (Cincinnati: Standard, 1914), 476.

5   Cited by Kenneth E. Bailey, *Through Peasant Eyes*, (Grand Rapids: Eerdmans, 1979), 41-42.
6   William Barclay, *The Gospel of Luke* (The Daily Study Bible Series, Rev. Ed.; Philadelphia: Westminster, 1975), 139.
7   Isn't it interesting that those who fault the man who fell among robbers for traveling alone never blame the Samaritan for doing exactly the same thing?
8   L. D. Hurst and J. B. Green, "Priest, Priesthood," *Dictionary of Jesus and the Gospels* (eds. Joel B. Green, Scot McKnight and I. Howard Marshall; Downers Grove: InterVarsity Press, 1992), 636.
9   Bailey, *Peasant Eyes*, 43. Contra Snodgrass, who states that many of the priests and Levites were actually poor. Klyne Snodgrass, *Stories With Intent* (Grand Rapids: Eerdmans, 2008), 354.
10 Bailey, *Peasant Eyes*, 43.
11 Bailey, *Peasant Eyes*, 43-44. Bailey also cites the passage in Sirach 12. The italics in the quote are Bailey's.
12 Sometimes called the "Retribution Dogma," it is reflected in Luke 13:2; John 9:2; Acts 28:4.
13 Henry S. Gehman, ed., *The New Westminster Dictionary of the Bible* (Philadelphia: Westminster, 1970), "Levites," 559.
14 Robert H. Stein, *An Introduction to the Parables of Jesus* (Philadelphia: Westminster, 1981), 56, 123, 127.
15 Perhaps the introduction of a Samaritan in this parable, in addition to the social, political, religious and racial issues it raised, also served as a gentle rebuke to James and John who in the previous chapter wished to call fire down on a Samaritan village. (Luke 9:54)
16 The word "Jew" is derived from Judea, the Southern Kingdom.
17 Joseph Halévy believed that when Jesus originally told this parable it was not a Samaritan who helped the injured man, but an Israelite. He also charged that as Luke recorded Jesus' story he changed the ethnicity of the hero in order to make it more palatable to a

Gentile audience. Bernard Brandon Scott, *Hear Then a Parable: A Commentary on the Parables of Jesus* (Minneapolis: Fortress, 1989), 199-200. Halévy's view has little support, however. It should be noted that even among Jesus Seminar participants (who tend to be on the liberal side of the spectrum) this verse's authenticity was rated as "authentic," by 60% of participants, with another 29% concluding it is "probably authentic." Peter Rhea Jones, *Studying the Parables of Jesus* (Macon, GA: Smyth and Helwys Publishing, 1999), 294.

18   Leon Morris, *Luke* (Tyndale New Testament Commentaries, Vol. 3; Grand Rapids: Eerdmans, 1989), 207.

19   Bailey, *Peasant Eyes,* 50.

20   John Nolland, *Luke 9:21-18:34* (Word Biblical Commentary, Vol. 35b; Gen. Eds. David A. Hubbard and Glen W. Baker; Dallas: Word, 1989), 596. The need for inns in the ancient world grew out of the Roman road system made possible by the *Pax Romana*. If one day's labor paid for a week's worth of lodging, then the rates were quite low when compared to contemporary standards!

Chapter 5: The Answer and Some Applications

1   Michael Lodahl, "On Being the Neighbor: How John Wesley's Reading of the Parable of the Good Samaritan May Cultivate Loving People," (Edwin Crawford Lectureship, Northwest Nazarene University; February 5, 2009), 5. http://wesley.nnu.edu/fileadmin/imported_site/wesley_conferences/2009/On_Being_the_Neighbor; downloaded December 3, 2012.

2   Some rabbis in Jesus' day taught that if a wall should happen to collapse on a Sabbath trapping a man underneath the rubble, that they should clear away just enough debris to determine whether the man was a Jew or a Gentile. If he was Jewish, he should be rescued. If he was Gentile he should be left to suffer. William Barclay, *And Jesus*

   Said (Edinburgh: Church of Scotland Youth Committee, reprint 1965), 77.
3. Lodahl, 4.
4. Timothy Keller, *The Prodigal God* (New York: Penguin, 2008), 127.
5. Craig L. Blomberg, *Preaching the Parables: From Responsible Interpretation to Powerful Proclamation* (Grand Rapids: Baker Academic, 2004), 61.
6. James D. Smart, *The ABC's of Christian Faith* (Philadelphia: Westminster, 1968), 27.
7. M. Daniel Carroll R., "Immigration: What Does the Bible Say?" *Christian Standard* (June 17, 2012), 4.
8. Brad Knickerbocker, "Illegal Immigrants in the US: How Many Are There?" (*Christian Science Monitor*, May 16, 2006).
9. Alan F. H. Wisdom, "Immigration: What's a Christian to Think?" *Christian Standard* (June 17, 2012), 6.
10. Wisdom, 6.
11. Martin Luther, "Secular Authority: To What Extent It Should Be Obeyed," *Works of Martin Luther* (Vol. 3.; transl. Henry Cole; London: Simkin and Marshall, 1826), 231-250.
12. Summing up Luther on this point, Bainton writes "The natural man, when not involved for himself, has enough integrity and insight to administer the state in accord with justice, equity, and even magnanimity. These are civil virtues. But the Church inculcates humility, patience, long-suffering, and charity—the Christian virtues—attainable even approximately only by those endowed by grace, and consequently not to be expected from the masses." Ronald H. Bainton, *Here I Stand* (New York: Meridian, 1995), 188.
13. Those who allegorically place Jesus in the role of the Good Samaritan sometimes also understand the victim to be Old Testament Israel. Klyne Snodgrass, *Stories With Intent* (Grand Rapids: Eerdmans, 2008), 348.

[14] William Barclay, *The Gospel of Matthew*, Vol. 1. (The Daily Study Bible Series, Rev. Ed.; Philadelphia: Westminster, 1975), 103.

Chapter 6: Approaching the Parable of the Prodigal Son

[1] Robert H. Stein, *Luke* (The New American Commentary, Vol. 24; Nashville: Broadman, 1992), 182.

[2] Craig L. Blomberg, *Matthew* (The New American Commentary, Vol. 22; Nashville: Broadman, 1992), 340.

[3] Jesus often taught from a seated position. (Matthew 5:1; 13:2; Luke 4:20; John 8:2) Jesus' posture in Luke 15, however, is not recorded.

[4] Fred Craddock, *Luke* (Interpretation: A Bible Commentary for Teaching and Preaching; Louisville: John Knox, 1990), 186.

[5] Matthew's account of this parable can be found in Matthew 18:12-14. There are some significant variations between the accounts of Matthew and Luke, causing some to conclude that while similar they should be considered as two separate stories. Snodgrass gives a brief, but excellent treatment on this issue. Klyne Snodgrass, *Stories With Intent* (Grand Rapids: Eerdmans, 2008), 98-104.

[6] To be "lost" in all three of the parables in Luke 15 means to be "out of place," much akin to losing your car keys. The emphasis is on the lost object not being where it belongs. Within this context it does not imply damnation or punishment.

[7] Stein, 404.

[8] William Barclay, *The Gospel of Luke* (The Daily Study Bible Series, Rev. Ed; Philadelphia: Westminster, 1975), 202. Jeremias and Bailey have also promoted the idea that the lost coin might have been a part of a bridal veil, but Snodgrass finds the evidence to be sketchy and unconvincing. Besides, to drill a hole in a coin to make it usable on a veil would significantly lessen its value. Klyne Snodgrass, *Stories With Intent* (Grand Rapids: Eerdmans, 2008), 114.

9. The friends and neighbors (*tas philas kai geitonas*) are both in the feminine form.
10. Cited by William J. Richardson, *The Restoring Father* (Cincinnati: Standard, 1987), 12.
11. T. W. Manson, *The Sayings of Jesus* (London: SCM, 1949), 262.
12. F. F. Bruce, "Interpretation (Biblical)," *Baker's Dictionary of Theology* (Everett F. Harrison, ed.; Grand Rapids: Baker, 1960), 293.
13. Timothy Keller, *The Prodigal God* (New York: Penguin, 2008), xvii.

Chapter 7: The Seduction of Sin

1. Contra Eta Linnemann, who believes that requesting a share of an inheritance before the death of the testator was not unusual. Eta Linnemann, *Parables of Jesus: Introduction and Exposition* (New York: Harper and Row, 1967), 75. Wilhelm Michaelis takes the matter even further by arguing that the father must have been proud to hear that his younger son wanted to strike out on his own. It was only after his son had moved out of the house that temptation came his way and he started making poor decisions. Wilhelm Michaelis, *Die Gleichnisse Jesu* (Hamburg: Furche, 1956), 138.
2. John MacArthur, *The Prodigal Son* (Nashville: Nelson, 2008), 48.
3. Kenneth E. Bailey, *Poet & Peasant* (Grand Rapids: Eerdmans, 1976), 168.
4. Timothy Keller, *The Prodigal God* (New York: Penguin, 2008), 23.
5. In the context of Deuteronomy, the father has two wives and loves one more than the other. Regardless, the principle of primogeniture still applies.
6. Adolf Deissmann, *Bible Studies* (Edinburgh: T&T Clark, 1901), 230.
7. We can readily see how dispersing assets before death is fraught with danger. As such, it was not generally recommended. (Sirach 33:19-23)

⁸ The wisdom of the father's acquiescence to his younger son's demand is not an issue in this parable. While some have criticized the father for foolishly dividing his estate, we should remember that this parable, like all parables, is a work of fiction. Had the father said no to his younger son there would have been no story left to tell!

⁹ Matthew 25:24-25; 26:31; Mark 14:27; Luke 1:51; John 11:52. Later in the Parable of the Prodigal Son the word *squander* will appear again (Luke 15:30, NIV), but it will be based on a different Greek word.

¹⁰ Many if not most of the Pharisees and teachers of the law who first heard this story would disagree, holding that the famine might well be God's retribution for the younger son's sinful behavior. MacArthur, *Prodigal Son*, 64-67.

¹¹ Acts 16:37-38; 22:25-29; 23:27

¹² While he may have had scruples about tending unclean pigs, we wonder what misgivings he might have had about spending his father's money on prostitutes. (Luke 15:30) It was hunger that brought him to his senses. What role guilt might have played over his involvement with prostitutes is not mentioned. (Luke 15:17-20a)

¹³ *Baba Kamma* 82b as cited in Leon Morris, *Luke* (Tyndale New Testament Commentaries, Vol. 3; Grand Rapids: Eerdmans, 1988), 264.

¹⁴ R. C. H. Lenski, *The Interpretation of St. Luke's Gospel* (Minneapolis: Augsburg, 1946), 811. This interpretation, while plausible and has many supporters, isn't required by the text. Luke uses the same word in Acts 8:29 to describe the Spirit calling Philip to "join himself" to the Ethiopian eunuch's chariot. In this case Philip was certainly a welcome visitor. Other Lukan examples of both welcome and unwelcome "joining" include Luke 10:11; Acts 5:13; 9:26; and 10:28.

¹⁵ William J. Richardson, *The Restoring Father* (Cincinnati: Standard, 1987), 18.

16. Cited by Halford E. Luccock, *Studies in the Parables of Jesus* (New York: Abingdon, 1917), 21. The Winston Churchill quoted was no relation to the British Prime Minister of the same name.
17. Richard L. Rohrbaugh, "A Dysfunctional Family and It's Neighbors (Luke 15:11b-32)," in *Jesus and His Parables* (George Shillington, Ed.; Edinburgh: T&T Clark, 1997), 141-164. Rohrbaugh interprets the father's unwillingness to stand up to his son as a symptom of codependency. In his view, the party that takes place at the end of the parable is not to welcome his son home as much as it is to keep up appearances with the neighbors.
18. The father had divided his property (*bios*) between his two sons. (Luke 15:12) If it is true that money is "coined life," then there is not always a clear distinction between a person's life and his property. Thus, to "make a living" is to earn an income.
19. Carolyn Osiek, "Slavery in the Second Testament World," *Biblical Theology Bulletin* 22 (1992): 174.
20. There are a few exceptionally rare cases of a slave in antebellum America negotiating such an arrangement with his master. For an example, see Orville V. Burton, *The Age of Lincoln* (New York: Hill and Wang, 2007), 39.
21. Everett Ferguson, *Backgrounds of Early Christianity* (2nd Ed.; Grand Rapids: Eerdmans, 1993), 56-57.

Chapter 8: The Role of Repentance

1. Courtney Love, http://www.quotesea.com/quotes/by/courtney-love; downloaded October 5, 2011.
2. The younger son didn't need to be told how miserable he was. He already knew. Many contemporary preachers confuse sermons about sin with the "Good News." A person's sin is not good news. Alexander Campbell noted that "The gospel being glad tidings of great joy to all people, is not preached to sinners in order to produce pain, sorrow,

regret, conviction, condemnation ... [but] prepares the sinner to appreciate the value, the grace, the mercy, and compassion of our God, of our Lord and Savior, who at just this point commands us to change our views, feelings, conduct and position—all embraced in the word *metanoia* [repentance]." Alexander Campbell, *Millennial Harbinger* (September, 1854), 490-491.

3 Joachim Jeremias, *The Parables of Jesus* (New York: Scribner's, 1963), 130. Contra Hultgren and others, who question the sincerity of the younger son. Was his misery caused by his sense of sin or by his destitution? Perhaps he said what he said in an attempt to manipulate his father. Arland J. Hultgren, *The Parables of Jesus: A Commentary* (Grand Rapids: Eerdmans, 2002), 76. I have sided with those who believe true repentance had taken place, for to add a dimension of deceit at this point in the narrative seems to work against the point of the parable.

4 Some ancient Greek philosophers believed that under extreme stress the soul and body would actually part from one another. When this happened, a person was considered "beside himself." Jordan Almond, "Beside Himself," *Dictionary of Word Origins* (Secaucus, NJ: Carol Publishing, 1998). It is in this vein that I interpret the Prodigal Son as needing to come to grips with his identity, "for if he didn't he would always be away from himself."

5 John Killinger, *For God's Sake, Be Human* (Waco: Word, 1970), 17.

6 The word *orientation* comes from the idea of facing in the direction of the Orient, or eastward for most of western civilization. Since the sun also rises in the east, it is a direction that will help you find your bearings. In a broader sense, however, to be oriented (such after attending an "orientation meeting") means that you have learned how things operate.

7 William J. Richardson, *The Restoring Father* (Cincinnati: Standard, 1987), 30.

8   The words "against heaven" (*eis ton ouranon*) can also be translated "to heaven." In other words, "his sins were so many as to reach heaven." More likely, however, is that "heaven" refers to God. Walter L. Liefeld, *Matthew, Mark, Luke* (The Expositor's Bible Commentary, Vol. 8; Frank E. Gaebelein, Gen. Ed.; Grand Rapids: Zondervan, 1984), 984.

9   Gustaf Dalman, *The Words of Jesus in the Light of Post-Biblical Jewish Writings and the Aramaic Language* (Transl. D. M. Kay; Eugene, OR: Wipf and Stock, 1997) 204f. See Matthew 5:33-37 for another example.

10 Jeremias acknowledges the similarities between God and the father in this parable—traits such as goodness, grace, mercy, and abounding love. Still, he resists identifying them too closely with each other in allegorical fashion, for the younger son's statement that he had sinned against *both* heaven and his father shows a distinction between the two. Joachim Jeremias, *Rediscovering the Parables* (New York: Scribner's, 1966), 101, 103.

11 Stein believes this should not be interpreted in terms of the prodigal's legal status, but rather his relational status with his father. He suggests a better understanding of this verse is "A father like you deserves better than a son like me." Robert H. Stein, *Luke* (The New American Commentary, Vol. 24; Nashville: Broadman, 1992), 406.

12 William O. E. Oesterley, *The Gospel Parables in the Light of Their Jewish Background* (London: SPCK, 1936), 186. Contra Joseph H. Heinemann, "The Status of the Laborer in Jewish Law and Society in the Tannaitic Period," *Hebrew Union College Annual* 25 (1954), 263-325. Heinemann argues that the younger son's free status means that he would be able to keep whatever income he might receive from his labor, perhaps with a view of paying his father back someday.

¹³ Alexander Campbell wrote of this spiritual predicament, a paraphrase of which goes something like this: "If God hates sin and I am a sinner, then God must hate me. What's more, if God hates me, then how can I ever be reconciled to him?" If an estranged person is going to find harmony with his heavenly father, he must first come to grips with the truth that "God is love." Alexander Campbell, *Millennial Harbinger*, (August 5, 1833), 338-339.

¹⁴ Richardson, 40-42.

Chapter 9: In the Grip of Grace

¹ It is often argued that the prodigal's lost condition was already firmly established before he demanded his share of the inheritance, making his departure from home merely a symptom of his lostness. This view coincides with the idea that the elder son who remained at home was equally lost in this parable.

² The verb used for compassion is *splanchnizomai*, which means to have your bowels moved. In other words, the father was deeply moved emotionally. Elsewhere the NIV translates this word as having "your heart go out" to someone. (Luke 7:13) The need for a restroom is not implied!

³ Cited by Kenneth E. Bailey, *Poet and Peasant* (Grand Rapids: Eerdmans, 1976), 181.

⁴ This same idiom also appears in Acts 20:37, where the Ephesian elders bid Paul farewell.

⁵ The verb *katephilsen* may mean that the father tenderly kissed him, or more likely that he kissed him repeatedly.

⁶ Craig S. Keener, "Kissing," *Dictionary of New Testament Background* (ed. Craig A. Evans and Stanley Porter; Downers Grove: IVP, 2000). Of course, in the ancient world kissing was not reserved for family members. Kissing took on a broad role of greeting, much as a handshake does in western culture today. Early Christians were

admonished to "Greet one another with a holy kiss." (Romans 16:16; 1 Corinthians 16:20; 2 Corinthians 13:12; 1 Thessalonians 5:26; 1 Peter 5:14) Judas Iscariot used this form of greeting to betray Christ. (Matthew 26:48-49; Mark 14:44-45; Luke 22:47-48)

[7] Some ancient manuscripts include the words "Make me like one of your hired men" in verse 21. In all probability these words were not in Luke's original text but were added later, either deliberately or accidently. In any case, it doesn't change the father's delight to have his son home. It only becomes a question as to what point the father interrupts his son. Bruce M. Metzger, *A Textual Commentary on the Greek New Testament* (2nd Ed; New York: American Bible Society, 1998), 139.

[8] There are four different words for "robe" used in the New Testament. In the Gospels, *stolē* denotes the robes worn by scribes (Mark 12:38; Luke 20:46) and the robe worn by an angel at the empty tomb of Jesus (Mark 16:5). In practical usage, it was the kind of robe that a host would give to an honored guest.

[9] A. T. Robertson, *Word Pictures in the New Testament*, (Vol. 2; Nashville: Broadman, 1930), 211.

[10] As told by William Barclay, *The Gospel of Luke* (The Daily Bible Study Series, Rev. Ed.; Philadelphia: Westminster, 1975), 205.

[11] Pontius Pilate used such a seal on the tomb of Jesus. (Matthew 27:66) In Revelation 5:1 God himself holds a scroll sealed with seven seals. Jesus is declared to be worthy to break the seals and to open the scroll, demonstrating that he has equal authority with God.

[12] Barclay, 205.

[13] William Barclay, *And Jesus Said* (Edinburgh: Church of Scotland Youth Committee, Reprint 1965), 176.

[14] Contra John Nolland, who holds that while the ring signifies honor, there is no reason to believe this particular ring is a signet ring. Therefore, he says that no plenipotentiary power is necessarily

implied. John Nolland, *Luke 9:21-18:34* (Word Biblical Commentary, Vol. 35b; Gen Eds. David A. Hubbard and Glen W. Baker; Dallas, TX: Word, 1993), 785.

[15] Arthur C. Jones, *The Spirituals Project: "Spirituals as Expressions of Protest"* (Denver: University of Denver, 2004), http://ctl.du.edu/spirituals/freedom/protest.cfm. Downloaded March 31, 2012.

[16] The word that Jesus uses for "fattened" is the verbal adjective of *siteuō*, or "to feed with wheat." The calf was grain fed. Robertson, 211.

[17] Bailey, *Poet and Peasant*, 186-187.

[18] LeRoy Lawson, *The Lord of Promises* (Cincinnati: Standard, 1983), 39.

[19] Desmond Tutu, *God Has a Dream: A Vision of Hope for Our Time* (New York: Doubleday, 2004), 36.

[20] Joachim Jeremias warns against pushing this analogy too far, holding that this parable is not an allegory, but rather "a story taken from life." Therefore, he says we cannot equate the father in the parable with God. Furthermore, the parable itself holds the father to be someone other than God. (Luke 15:18, 21) Still, he admits that the father and God share the common characteristics of goodness, grace, mercy, and abounding love. Joachim Jeremias, *Rediscovering the Parables* (New York: Scribner's, 1966), 101, 103.

[21] Contra Keller, who holds that there is an implied atonement in this parable. The father, in essence, saw that the price of his younger son's return would be paid through the disruption and loss of a sizable portion of his estate. Because the father had already divided his estate between both sons, he was no longer the sole owner. As a result, it was the older son who would be forced to pay the "atoning price" of having his younger brother restored. Timothy Keller, *The Prodigal God* (New York: Penguin, 2008), 92-94.

[22] In contrast, McGee argues that "This [parable] is not the picture of a sinner who gets saved," for the prodigal was a son *before* he left

home. Rather, it is a parable featuring how a backsliding son can be restored to fellowship. J. Vernon McGee, *Luke* (Glendale, CA: Griffin Printing, 1983), 179-180.

23   Robert H. Stein, *Luke* (The New American Commentary, Vol. 24; Nashville: Broadman, 1992), 410.

24   Some scholars believe that this parable did, in fact, originally end at verse 24. They believe that what we read in Luke 15:11-32 is actually a compilation of two separate parables told by Jesus, edited together by Luke. Others hold that 15:11-24 is the original parable told by Jesus, with 15:25-32 being created by Luke himself to fit the overall "lost and found" theme of chapter 15. However, the parable begins "There was a man who had two sons," so clearly both sons have a role to play in the story, suggesting a unified whole. In addition, the consistent role of the father throughout the parable also points to a single story. Fred Craddock, *Luke* (Interpretation: A Bible Commentary for Preaching and Teaching; Louisville: John Knox, 1990), 187.

Chapter 10: Grumbling About Grace

1   The word for music is *symphōnia*, which shows a combination of sounds in harmony with each other. Sometimes translated as dulcimer or bagpipe, it is the basis for the English word *symphony*. Vincent considers this "concerted music." Marvin R. Vincent, *Word Studies in the New Testament* (Vol. 1; Grand Rapids: Eerdmans, 1887), 390.

2   The word *hugiainō* is the basis for the English word *hygiene*. Strictly speaking, it refers to someone's physical health (Matthew 8:13; Luke 5:31), but it can also be used to describe sound or healthy doctrine (1 Timothy 1:10; 2 Timothy 4:3; Titus 1:9; 2:1, etc.) William F. Arndt and F. Wilbur Gingrich, *A Greek-English Lexicon of the New Testament and Other Early Christian Literature* (4th Ed; Transl. Walter

Bauer; Chicago: University of Chicago Press, 1952), "*Hugiainō*," 839-840. Physical health is linked to spiritual health in 3 John 2, where the Apostle writes "May your body be as healthy as your soul." (Author's paraphrase).

3 Fred Craddock, *Luke* (Interpretation: A Bible Commentary for Preaching and Teaching: Louisville: John Knox, 1990), 188.

4 Craddock, 188.

5 The word is *orgē*, which suggests "a settled or abiding condition of mind, frequently with a view to taking revenge." *Orgē* is differentiated from *thumos* in that *thumos* is more of an outburst of anger that subsides relatively quickly, while *orgē* tends to fester. W. E. Vine, *An Expository Dictionary of New Testament Words* (Vol. 1; Old Tappan, NJ: Revell, 1966), "Anger," 55-56.

6 Norval Geldenhuys, *Commentary on the Gospel of Luke* (Grand Rapids: Eerdmans, 1951), 410.

7 Bailey interprets this boast as evidence that the guests are definitely listening to the older son's protest and that the son is "playing to the gallery." Bailey, *Poet and Peasant* (Grand Rapids: Eerdmans, 1976), 197.

8 The word for goat (*eriphon*) is in the diminutive form. This is a young goat, a kid.

9 Hultgren estimates that goat meat was worth about one tenth of that of a cow. Arland J. Hultgren, *The Parables of Jesus: A Commentary* (Grand Rapids: Eerdmans, 2000), 81.

10 Despite my disparaging comments about goat meat, it is nevertheless consumed by about 75% of the world's population and is growing in popularity in America. Because it is so low in fat, it must be cooked slowly at a low temperature and kept from drying out. See http://www.lazyjboergoats.com/id13.html (Downloaded April 18, 2012).

11 Leon Morris, *Luke* (Tyndale New Testament Commentaries, Vol. 3; Grand Rapids: Eerdmans, 1989), 287.

12. The Greek word is *katathagōn*. While we would say the father's property was "eaten up," the Greek term literally means "eaten down." Vincent, Vol. 1, 391.
13. The word for prostitute is *pornē*, from the word *pernēmi* (to sell). Vine, Vol. 2; 195-196. It is also the root of the English word *pornography*.
14. A. T. Robertson, *Word Pictures in the New Testament* (Vol. 2; Nashville: Broadman, 1930), 213.
15. William J. Richardson, *The Restoring Father* (Cincinnati: Standard, 1987), 24.
16. Craddock, 188.
17. The good news for Israel is that they can be now be saved on the same basis as the Gentiles are: through faith in Jesus Christ. (Romans 11:26-27)

Chapter 11: The Result of Reconciliation

1. A. T. Robertson, *Word Pictures in the New Testament* (Vol. 2; Nashville: Broadman, 1930), 213. Note that the father calls his older son *teknon* (child) rather than *huios* (son), the word which the older son used earlier to apply to the prodigal. (Luke 15:30) While some translations don't draw a distinction between the two terms, Vine observes that *teknon* emphasizes the importance of birth, while *huios* emphasizes "the dignity and character of the relationship." V. E. Vine, *An Expository Dictionary of New Testament Words* (Vol. 1; Old Tappan, NJ: Revell, 1966), "child," 187. Since the father says that "everything I have is yours," he chooses the word *teknon* in order to stress his older son's legal birthright. Thus, he implies that the older son has nothing to fear by his father's celebration. He will not miss out on anything that is rightfully and legally his.
2. The word *pantote* (always) is rather elastic in terms of past, present and future applications. For examples, see John 18:20 (past); 1

Thessalonians 5:15, 16; 2 Timothy 3:7; Hebrews 7:25 (present); and John 6:34; 1 Thessalonians 4:17 (future).

3   Knox translates this phrase as "Everything that I have is already yours." *The Holy Bible* (transl. Ronald Knox; New York: Sheed and Ward, 1954), Luke 15:31.

4   Luke's use of the word *edei* is repeatedly connected with a "divine must" in his gospel. For example, "The Son of Man *must* suffer many things ... and *must* be killed and on the third day be raised to life." (Luke 9:22) In this way God's sovereignty over history is displayed. See Robert H. Stein, *Luke* (The New American Commentary, Vol. 24; Nashville: Broadman, 1992), 45-46. It is significant that such a strong word would be used here in Luke 15:32. To exercise joy in welcoming someone back into God's family is not just a nice thing to do. It is a "divine must."

5   Francois Bovon and Gregoire Rouiller, *Exegesis: Problems of Method and Exegesis in Reading (Genesis 22 and Luke 15)* (Pittsburg: Pickwick, 1978), 203.

6   Herbert C. Hoover, "Speech on Rugged Individualism," given in New York City on October 22, 1928. See http://www.pinzler.com/ushistory/ruggedsupp.html (Downloaded May 14, 2012). Hoover argued that an expanded federal government, which may be necessary in times of war, undermines personal freedom if continued after the war is over. Fifteen days after delivering this campaign speech Hoover was elected the 31st president of the United States. Nearly a year later the stock market crashed ushering in the Great Depression.

7   Julie A. Gorman, *Community That is Christian* (Wheaton: Victor, 1993), 60.

8   Gorman, 61.

9   Rick Warren, *The Purpose Driven Life* (Grand Rapids: Zondervan, 2002), 17.

10. Marshall notes a possible exception in the case of the Ethiopian eunuch in Acts 8:39. I. Howard Marshall, *Luke: Historian and Theologian* (Grand Rapids: Zondervan, 1971), 212.
11. Marshall, 214.
12. In most English translations the father repeats himself word for word. The Greek text, however, shows a slight, insignificant variation. For a fuller treatment of being dead vs. alive and lost vs. found, see chapter nine.
13. Carol J. Miller, *Good News for All: The Gospel of Luke* (Kerygma Program Sample; www.kerygma.com/courses/elective/GoodNews-GospelofLukeRBpdf), Downloaded May 17, 2012.
14. Both the divestiture and reinvestiture ceremonies are described by Karl Heinrich Rengsdorf, *Die Re-Investitur des verlorenen Sohnes in der Gleichniserzählung Jesu: Luk 15, 11-32* (Köhn: Westerdeutscher Verlag, 1967).
15. See Matthew 9:10-13; 11:19; Mark 2:15-17; and Luke 5:29-32 for other occasions when Jesus was criticized for associating with "sinners."
16. While the concept of "tough love" has been practiced for centuries, it was first formally articulated by Bill Milliken in 1968. See Bill Milliken, *Tough Love* (Spire Books: Old Tappan, 1971).

Chapter 12: Morals to the Stories

1. On other occasions Jesus was much less diplomatic, such as when he called the Pharisees and teachers of the law hypocrites, sons of hell, blind guides and snakes. (Matthew 23:1-37) Also note that Jesus took direct physical action when he overturned the tables in the Temple (Matthew 21:12-13; Mark 11:15-18; Luke 19:45-46; John 2:13-16)
2. Kenneth E. Bailey, *Poet and Peasant* (Grand Rapids: Eerdmans, 1976), 72-73. While retaining Bailey's structure, I have paraphrased his wording.

[3] Bailey, *Poet and Peasant*, 160. Again, I have paraphrased Bailey's wording.

[4] I'm using the term "salvation" (*sōtēria*) in the sense of being made whole. It means that body, soul and spirit and all healthy and functioning together in harmony. From a Christian perspective, spiritual wholeness means that a person has been reconciled to God through Jesus Christ and thus is "saved" from an existence apart from God.

[5] While not turning a blind eye to any legitimate need, Paul offers this priority for local church benevolence: "Therefore, as we have opportunity, let us do good to all people, especially to those who belong to the family of believers." (Galatians 6:10)

[6] This quote has been utilized by and attributed to many different authors.

[7] Maurice Wagner, *The Sensation of Being Somebody* (Grand Rapids: Zondervan, 1975), 179-180.